I

The Writer Within

The Writer Within

LARY BLOOM

CB

CONTEMPORARY
BOOKS
CHICAGO

Library of Congress Cataloging-in-Publication Data

Bloom, Lary
    The writer within : how to discover your own ideas, get them
on paper, and sell them for publication / Lary Bloom.
      p.   cm.
   ISBN 0-8092-4057-2 (pbk.)
   1. Authorship.   I. Title.
PN153.B57   1991
808'.02—dc20   91-33987
                                                      CIP

The author is grateful for permission to reprint from several
sources, including *Letters to a Young Doctor*, by Richard Selzer,
Simon & Schuster, copyright 1982; *Short Voyages*, by Stephen
Jones, W. W. Norton & Company, Inc., copyright 1985; *Mostly True
Confessions*, by Jean Gonick, Random House, copyright 1986;
Tropic, the Sunday magazine of the *Miami Herald*, "Zepp's Last
Stand," by Madeleine Blais, copyright 1979; *Beacon*, the Sunday
magazine of the *Akron Beacon Journal*, "Together," by James Ricci,
copyright 1972; *Northeast*, the Sunday magazine of the *Hartford
Courant* (several pieces).

Cover design by Georgene Sainati

Published by Contemporary Books, Inc.
180 North Michigan Avenue, Chicago, Illinois 60601
Manufactured in the United States of America
International Standard Book Number: 0-8092-4057-2

To Heather Price, who found her voice at fourteen;
Martha Munzer, who found hers at eighty-one;
and Dominic Koo, who found his before it was too late.

Contents

Acknowledgments

Humorist Colin McEnroe offered unbrief commentary on the soul of wit. Anne Longley revealed the source of her magic in getting famous people to sit for interviews. Jean Gonick was only too happy to recall a dreadful moment in her life—a moment that gave birth to her writing career. Phyllis Rose talked freely of how she turns notions into essays. Steve Kemper kept calling back with more thoughts on how to bug editors.

For such illumination and candor, I am also indebted to John Katzenbach, Nancy Pappas, Madeleine Blais, John Dorschner, Stephen Jones, David Morse, Patricia Weiss, Joel Lang, Bob Sudyk, Deborah Geigis, Steve Metcalf, Nancy Slonim Aronie, Annie Dillard, Gary Dorsey, Fred Mann, James Ricci, and Jeffrey Klein.

I am grateful to Jan Winburn, my longtime associate editor at *Northeast*, who was the originating editor on many of the writing projects examined on these pages; and to Michael E. Waller, editor of the *Hartford Courant*, a champion of Sunday magazine journalism.

I appreciate, too, the wise counsel provided by the editors of this book, Nancy Crossman and Gerilee Hundt.

Finally, there are the two inspiring Elizabeths. The idea for the book emerged at a lunch with Elizabeth Frost Knappman, my literary agent. Elizabeth A. Gwillim, my literary wife, offered advice and comfort in abundance.

৯১ 1 ৫৫

The Universal Gift

A Brief Argument on Behalf of Your Possibilities

A book about writing might logically begin with Mrs. H., who as far as I know never wrote anything for publication in her extensive lifetime. Mrs. H., however, left indelible impressions on children. One by one, we were summoned from class to the hallway, where an upright piano had been rolled, to attend her movable auditions for sixth-grade chorus. We were each asked for our best arpeggio, and although my vocal performance exceeded any private expectations, it was greeted with an unfavorable review ("not quite right") and I was summarily banished to a nonsinging life.

I did not know it at the time, but I had learned my first enduring lesson in having, or not having, talent. A person could either sing, or he couldn't. Perhaps I could be taught to play piano—and soon thereafter I was taught by a Miss F.—but I never aspired to carry a tune in public. Even piano playing had its limits. Miss F. specialized in notes, not theory. I could address the ivories with some competency, even felicity, but if you had asked me about the principles behind a sonata, I would have shrugged, silently deferring to the interpretations of the gifted.

My musical horizons did not change until nearly forty years after that school audition, when Mr. E., a jazz piano teacher, argued that I could learn not only theory but improvisation. It was neither my training nor my "talent" that seemed to convince him of this as much as my intense interest; by now I had grown to love music so much, even as an outsider, that it had become a priority in what I began to understand was a finite lifetime. Music mattered to me in a way that writing and editing had always mattered. Therefore I could be taught. I would play a lot of wrong notes. I might occasionally perform for unimpressed ears. But, as I soon learned, I could do what Mr. E. predicted I would do. Moreover, I could provide my own vocal accompaniment, exhibiting a voice that had never been appreciated but, on the other hand, was certainly well rested.

I hesitate to carry this metaphor too far—the last thing I should do in the initial stages of this writing book is leave me, or you, semiappreciated at the piano bench—but it does serve to reveal certain underlying emotions common to all who would make music, or art, or who would write words. Confidence and competency are lifelong pursuits. And such pursuits are sometimes easily undermined by the negative assessments of others.

As you know, or as you will find, there is no shortage of negative reviews. And this proliferation is not limited to the arts; human nature seems to encourage those who possess influence over others to find the faults. An "expert" seems on far safer ground to point out shortcomings—because they can always be found—than to find the elusive, subjective, seemingly indefensible notion that somewhere inside the insecure novice is a sign of grand possibilities.

For more than twenty years as a magazine editor, I have made my living subscribing to the latter point of view. I believe that writing is an opportunity for anyone who commits to it, and I have taught hundreds to write well by gently helping them find their natural voices, and by publishing those voices. Some of these people arrived at my office with credentials, some with none. Some pecked at manual typewriters, some wrote on state-of-the-art word processors, and some used legal pads or notebooks. One novice was an eighty-one-year-old great grandmother when she started, another a seventy-four-year-old actress. One young man had dropped out of high school, and one fourteen-year-old girl had no real life experience except as an emotionally injured daughter of divorce. Some writers were community pillars, some locked away in prison. One was barely literate, a condition that contributed to his intermittently homeless station. Some eventually earned Pulitzer Prizes (including one writer who much earlier had been told by a prestigious newspaper that she had no talent), quite a few went on to write very good books, and some earned only the substantial prize of knowing they could do what was suspected they might never do. All were different yet all the same: they all had notions they might have something to say, that they might one day be published.

Yet the premise that anyone can write is not unqualified or simplistic, and it did not emerge overnight. It was, as writing is, a long process—fitful and rewarding, full of paradoxes and surprises—that began in a city known much more for the products of rubber factories than of literary mills. It began at a "dead end" in Akron, Ohio.

The news of Tib's death in the fall of 1971 had not been unexpected; this imposing, dapper man had lived for many years with a bad heart. Yet it is also accurate to say he possessed a good heart.

As my first mentor, Loren Tibbals had been encouraging in the way many seasoned newspaper hands had not. There were annoying things about Tib, certainly, such as the tours that lunch companions were obliged to take through downtown Akron as he deposited checks into four savings and loans because, he explained, "My wife and I don't want to exceed the FDIC indemnity limit in any one institution." Yet if demonstrations of unaccustomed wealth, a product of his most recent marriage, were boorish, his professional mannerisms were not. He sensed in me a fascination with what he did for a living, and he took a special interest in my growth.

Tib was editor of *Beacon*, the *Akron Beacon Journal*'s Sunday magazine. Actually, "magazine" may be misleading. In the tradition of most such publications of the time, "supplement" was more fitting. *Beacon* often seemed like a mere excuse to print undergarment ads from O'Neil's department store. Most of its content was provided by syndicate, and it therefore was geographically and spiritually remote. Tib knew that a better publication was possible, even if he had failed to express a vision for it. He supported my eagerness to explore a vision of my own that a traditional Sunday supplement could become a force in the community. The truth is, I had no adequate words to describe this vision, merely a feeling. The lack of persuasive vocabulary did not help in the argument for change. The Sunday editor, Tib's boss, saw *Beacon* in traditional terms; he thought it should be harmless, clever, and weightless. It should not offend in any way. In short, it should contain no real writing. In a city that faced the loss of its lifeblood industry, where, on one of its nearby campuses, Ohio National Guardsmen had fired at student protesters and had killed four of them, and where residents throughout the region suffered privately with the consequences of drugs or domestic violence or crime or poverty or treacheries of life that do not fit neatly into categories, the magazine was content to focus merrily on nuns playing tennis and giraffes from the London Zoo. There may have been life and death issues to plumb, but it seemed it would take more than Tib's influence and my instincts to get started.

When Tib's fifth heart attack turned out to be his last, I assumed that I would be asked to take over and to expand his work. But there was no word on a replacement. One day in desperation I stopped the Sunday editor in the hallway and asked for the job. He fidgeted, looked past me out into the newsroom, and said, "If I were you, I wouldn't want it. It's a dead end."

No space should be spent here describing the maneuvering required before Tib's proverbial green visor was passed down to me; suffice it to say that the paper's management also surmised something could be done beyond what they had thus far seen and read. In our provincial city, it was unlikely that they were inspired by or even aware of what had just happened in Manhattan, where a supplement called *New York* was the only surviving section of the distinguished but defunct *Herald Tribune*. They probably did not know the particulars of how writers such as

Tom Wolfe, Jimmy Breslin, and Pete Hamill and editors such as Clay Felker demonstrated the power of the "supplement" to make such a difference that readers would subscribe even if the remainder of the newspaper weren't wrapped around it. The editors in Akron were probably inattentive—likely even hostile—to the emerging and controversial industry phrase "the New Journalism," a narrative form of reporting that applied fiction techniques to nonfiction and yet purported to be more truthful, more illuminating, than so-called objective reporting.

And yet the editors in Akron, for whatever their reasons, decided that their magazine would no longer be the editors' graveyard. They allowed me to pursue that as yet undefined personal vision, an allowance that permitted some fairly embarrassing demonstrations of sophomoric tendencies but also allowed me the opportunity to do what I could do best; despite the delicate confidence levels of those who would write, I could forge a magazine worth reading, a magazine that mattered to its readers. And now, looking back more than two decades, after editing not only *Beacon* but *Tropic* at the *Miami Herald* and *Northeast* at the *Hartford Courant* (a magazine I started), it is abundantly clear that the vision was well worth pursuing—that it sought and found a way through journalism's "dead end," a dead end through which many rewarding lifetime literary journeys have begun.

This new territory, explored in New York, in the plains of Kansas (where Truman Capote researched *In Cold Blood*), and in provinces in northeastern Ohio, was the development of a new kind of literature, nonfiction that over the years has come to take its place alongside fiction as a primary medium. That's a modest judgment. Tom Wolfe, although not a neutral assessor of the genre he helped found, argues passionately on its behalf: "The literary history of the second half of the twentieth century will record that journalists not only took over the richness of American life as their domain, but also seized the high ground of literature itself." Wolfe's arguments were spelled out in a *Harper's* magazine article that explored the essence and origins of his bombshell novel, *The Bonfire of the Vanities*, and his belief that modern fiction and nonfiction should become indistinguishable to the extent that both must be based on passionate, bountiful, and flawless reporting.

There are those whom you will meet in this book whose work exemplifies that emerging school of writing; it is work that has been acknowledged in the highest circles. And nearly all the others, celebrated or not, can trace the beginnings of their fruitful careers, as Tom Wolfe can, to Sunday magazine projects.

Over this time, we have learned together many useful writing lessons. Those lessons are the essence of this book. To a large degree, the case-study method is employed; that is, I will take you inside the problem and present the writer's and editor's solution. In a word, this is a book of stories about story telling.

I am no fan of the customary forms of self-help writing. If you were to examine each of the well over a thousand issues of magazines I have produced over the years, you would note a dearth of advice about ridding your scalp of dandruff or improving your bowling score. My primary intention has been to illuminate the lives of readers by printing the essays, profiles, and narratives of passionate writers.

Such projects are not easy. You do not say, "Heed steps 1, 2, and 3, then swallow two magic pills, sing 'Follow the Yellow Brick Road,' take a nice nap, and then wake up a writer." Nor do I suggest that everyone is Mark Twain or Joan Didion or Ian Frazier. Natural world-class talent remains a rare commodity. Nor is my view a reflection of one editor's blindness to bad writing; I will offer evidence enough that writing allows for the commission of heinous misdemeanors.

But to the main point: Can anyone write? Can you write? Is the premise of this book a fair one? Yes, yes, and yes. As a Sunday magazine editor, I have been in a primary position to adjudge good writing, and to assess the power and potential of writers and of people who want to become writers.

In the last two decades, many Sunday magazines have come into the hands of editors who have sensed a special opportunity here, one found almost nowhere else in publishing. These are among the last of the general interest publications, the last of the "unmarketed" magazines, today's answer to the old *Saturday Evening Post, Look,* and *Collier's*—which were traditionally the training grounds for writers who went on to greater heights as novelists, biographers, or screenwriters. A selected group of Sunday magazines, by both default and design, have inherited this marketplace. In some ways they suffer from the same economic difficulties in that their audiences are too broad to attract narrowly focused advertisers. But because they arrive inside a Sunday paper they are subsidized, and their disadvantage from a marketing standpoint turns into a strong opportunity for writers.

The Sunday magazine has been an ideal training ground because the power of persuasion—necessary to meaningful writing—can be tested not on a narrow, think-alike readership but on many readers not naturally drawn to the subject matter or not necessarily in agreement with the point of view expressed by the writer.

My argument is not to champion the Sunday magazine so much as to say that it has been one of the few forums where periodical literature still thrives, where the primary purpose is not to sell walking shoes, gourmet frozen foods, or new cars. Our typical reader is not typical of anything. Our writers then must be the most enticing of writers. Yet when they have hooked readers, they are then licensed to seek the real essence of any good writing—the writer's truth. The beneficiaries of such work have been grateful readers, who in these days, when there is no shortage of words, are often moved by those that appear on our pages. Even the normally unsatisfiable press critic of *Punch* magazine, Roy Hattersley, observed, "At *Northeast*, they take words very seriously."

It is from this position that I have seen writing as not merely the province of prodigies but as a universal pursuit. Although I have told hundreds of writers that particular ideas may be unsuited for them, and although I have rejected thousands of pieces—all editors must become expert at this—I have never told a person who wanted to write that it wasn't possible to find a suitable project. I have never returned a piece because a person's qualifications didn't measure up—that because she wasn't a product of a Creative Writing curriculum she didn't have a prayer of cracking my literary lineup. I have never even thought to do such a thing. Pieces are rejected simply because in our judgment they do not work or are not suitable for us, not because the writer fails to produce evidence of proper blood-lines or training.

To put it on a more positive note, I have come to believe that, particularly in nonfiction, writing can certainly be taught to anyone who has enough genuine interest to learn. I believe what more than fifty years ago Brenda Ueland expressed in *If You Want to Write*, praised by Carl Sandburg as "the best writing book ever." Ueland argued, "Everybody is talented, original and has something important to say. . . ." It is simply a matter of proper teaching and encouragement. Where it begins is not with college degrees or consummate knowledge of all the great works of literature or with the recommendations of teachers who thought you clever, but only where Tib and I started so many years ago: with mere instinct. If there is something inside of you that yearns to be expressed, if you have ever told a good story or listened to one with eager ears, if you have an inherent interest in language and its power, if you are willing to suspend rules you may have learned or feelings of inadequacy long ago acquired, if you do not mind visiting intimate spiritual areas not yet explored, if you have an innate curiosity not easily satisfied, if you understand that in your formative years your failure to master The English Theme is no real indication of your ability or need in later years to communicate, if you are willing to under-stand that, while the pursuit is difficult and more than occasion-ally discouraging, sticking with it will pay off, if most of all you are willing to believe in what is possible—not in what isn't possible—you can be a writer.

⚘ 2 ⚘

A Writer's Mind

Who Gives You the License to Write?

A mind portrait of Dr. Richard Selzer, drawn from years as an admiring reader, proved unsuitable for the man I finally met. This giant of contemporary literature was not as physically imposing as I had imagined—he was of less than average height, fair complexion, and thin frame—although it was a presence quickly enlarged by an eager and interested smile. Still, he looked more like a mathematics professor than someone who all his life had confronted or interpreted the gravest of issues.

Here was a surgeon with surprises, not the least of which was an obvious cigarette addiction, for which he offered unsolicited commentary at lunch. "It is a rather embarrassing habit for a surgeon," he said, smiling, "but a venial sin, a sin of minor proportions." Yet the particulars of Richard Selzer's life that interested me that day many years ago were not his personal habits but a professional practice just as compulsive.

Until he turned forty, Selzer thought of himself strictly in medical terms; he practiced medicine and taught it at Yale. And then overnight—literally overnight—he became a writer.

He described to me his routine: surgery from 7:00 A.M. until 4:00 P.M. or thereabouts, dinner at 6:00, bed at 8:30, sleep until 1:00 A.M., write from 1:00 until 3:00—"the quietest part of the day"—and then nap until surgery called once again. It seemed an odd juxtaposition of habits, heightened by Selzer's undoc-

9

torly observations in his writing, in which he sometimes questioned his own methods and those of fellow practitioners. To many people outside the profession—people who thought of doctors as inapproachable and invulnerable—his writing was shockingly human, rich, and compelling. It revealed a doctor who was not afraid to be candid, who would not hide feelings behind a surgical mask or a wall of diplomas.

"My writing," he explained, "was a result of a burst of midlife-crisis energy. An inexplicable feeling came over me. I thought I might be coming down with something. It was an altered condition of my mind. I had no idea I was a writer, but suddenly I found myself writing the story of Jonah and the whale, convinced I knew more about what the lining of the whale's stomach looked like than the biblical authors knew. I've written every day since. I've had no choice. I am compelled to do it. I want to be a force for the rehumanization of medicine, which was once a purely technological pursuit."

I asked him if other doctors were critical of him, or if they felt threatened by his apparent betrayal of a noble society's secrets or jealous of his fame as a writer. He nodded. "But it doesn't really matter. There's no time for dinner parties any more."

Certainly as a writer or prospective writer you should read Selzer's remarkable volumes. And you should learn not only by the example of his prose but by his commitment to writing.

When he began his lonely early morning discipline, it was without encouragement from anyone. It was simply the result of an instinct, a drive, a voice in his head. He didn't necessarily go around calling himself a writer, didn't produce embossed business cards, and wasn't discouraged that his biography was never nominated for *Who's Who Among Larry King Interviewees*. He simply wrote. He wrote every morning, no matter how hard the surgery was the day before, nor how hard that of the next few hours promised to be. No matter what.

And he wrote without regard to consequence. In a piece that appeared in *Northeast* (and later in the volume of essays *Letters to a Young Doctor*), he told a story that described a doctor's most painful and private procedure: facing the family of a patient when there is no other prognosis but death, and when the pain is so pervasive that death—and quickly—is a blessing.

"I'll get rid of the pain," I tell his wife.

But there is no way to kill the pain without killing the man who owns it. Morphine to the lethal dose . . . and still he miaows and bays and makes other sounds like a boat breaking up in a heavy sea. I think his pain will live on long after he dies.

"Please," begs the old woman, his mother. "Do it now."

"To give him more would kill," I tell her.

"Then do it," she says. The face of the old woman is hoof-beaten, with intersecting curves of loose skin. Her hair is donkey brown, donkey gray.

[Selzer then goes on to describe the preparation for the upcoming "operation," and his conversation with the male patient.]

"Listen," I say, "I can get rid of the pain." The man's eyes regain their focus. His gaze is like a wound that radiates its pain outward so that all upon whom it fell would know the need of relief.

"With these," I hold up the syringes.

"Yes," he gasps. "Yes." . . .

"Go home," I say, repeating the words of the old woman. I turn off the light. In the darkness the contents of the bed are theoretical. No! I must watch. I turn the light back on. How reduced he is, a folded parcel, something chipped away until only its shape and a little breath are left. His impatient bones gleam as though to burst through the papery skin. I am impatient too, I want to get it over with, then step out into the corridor where the women are waiting. His death is like a jewel to them.

. . .

But this man will not die. The skeleton rouses from its stupor. The snout twitches as if to fend off a fly. What is it that shakes him like a gourd full of beans? The pulse returns, melts away, comes back again, and stays. The respirations are twelve, then fourteen. I have not done it. I did not murder him. I am innocent! . . .

The man in the bed swallows. His Adam's apple bobs slowly. It would be so easy to do it. Three minutes of pressure on the larynx. He is still not conscious, wouldn't feel it, wouldn't know. My thumb and finger-tips hover, land on his windpipe. My pulse beating on his neck, his in mine. I look back over my shoulder. No one. Two bar I.V. poles in a corner, their looped metal eyes witnessing. Do it! Fingers press. Again he swallows. Look back again. How closed the door is. And . . . my hands wilt. I cannot. It is not in me to do it. Not that way. The man's head swivels like an upturned fish. The squadron of ribs battles on. . . .

In the corridor the women lean against the wall, against each other. They are like a band of angels dispatched here to take possession of his body. It is the only thing that will satisfy them.

"He didn't die," I say. "He won't . . . or can't." They are silent.

"He isn't ready yet," I say.

"He is ready," the old woman says. "You ain't."

There is so much to say about this small excerpt—the color, the economy of language, the detail ("His impatient bones gleam as though to burst through the papery skin. . . ."), the images and metaphors ("The squadron of ribs battles on. . . ."), the feeling of being there, the insight into the doctor's dilemma. But the excerpt is included here to demonstrate that Selzer is just as dedicated to the writing craft as he is to the medical. That is, the profession of saving lives, as exalted as it is, is not necessarily more so than the critical practice of illuminating lives. Writing requires honesty and candor, even if it is the sort of honesty that the AMA would rather not introduce to laypeople. As an author, Selzer certainly took a risk. The very attempt to end the life of the patient under those circumstances could be seen at least as unethical and might have been viewed as criminal.

Richard Selzer offers a prime example of the anatomy of the Writing Mind. He demonstrates the need for listening to and recording that inner voice. And he personifies the dedication and courage that writing requires.

ᘯ ᘰ

You would be astonished by the legions who spend more time and energy saying they are writers than actually writing. I regularly run into people who promise that someday they will record fascinating episodes in their lives. *Someday* is a fantasy word. Someday never comes. Writers write not someday but today. Writers write because no other professional pursuit exceeds its importance. Writers write because the very process of writing— the intimacy between the writer and the piece of paper written on—is cleansing, inspiring, surprising, and illuminating, even if the process is sometimes difficult. Writers write because what they have to say matters, if not always to the world, at least to themselves. Writers write because instinctively they know that writing is self-discovery.

George F. Will, the columnist and bestselling author, says, "I write to find out what I think. I don't write to say what I know. I write to know things." Gary Dorsey, author of *The Fullness of Wings* and a former *Northeast* staff writer, says, "A lot of the excitement of writing is the act of discovery, of making sense out of chaos." And Al Burt, among the most elegant of Florida's writers, once told me that, "As a writer I really see myself as a cabinetmaker. What I try to do with each essay is to make the best cabinet I can." The writing life, certainly, is intellectual, physical, and spiritual adventure of the most intriguing order.

ᘯ ᘰ

I would not argue that everyone who wants to write should go to the extremes Susan Dodd sought in 1983, but her example is telling. Her first published piece, "On the Stump," was a short story in *Northeast* that was inspired by her experiences as the

former wife of a United States senator. Marital breakups generally are followed by economic hardship, but in Susan's case the
hardship was largely self-imposed. She decided to take the
opportunity to be alone—and to become a writer. She moved
from an eighteen-room Victorian house in Norwich, Connecticut, into a beachfront shack in Rhode Island that had little in the
way of amenities and no telephone. She told me of her intention
to live there on less than ten thousand dollars a year. It was a
way to focus on what was critical to her at that time in her life—
to see whether she could become a serious writer. Up until then
she had been unwilling to risk playing out her dream. Susan
later recalled in a *Hartford Courant* interview, "At an early age
I already knew writing was what I wanted to do. I think that's
why I didn't start until later, because knowing that there's one
thing only that you want desperately to do makes it scary. What
if you find out you can't? So it had been really easy to put it off."

The only updates I received on her progress in Rhode Island
were in the way of heavily rubber-stamped postcards and—even
happier evidence—new pieces to publish. In a very short time
Susan Dodd's fiction created a huge following in Connecticut,
and the reaction inspired her to greater goals. Writing from that
Rhode Island beach shack, she composed stories in the space of
two years that earned her the prestigious Iowa School of Letters
Award for Short Fiction, and then she went on to write several
well-received books.

There is, however, no need to purchase Rhode Island real
estate in your own effort to become a writer; the lesson here is
how important the craft of writing was to Susan. She did not
worry about life below the poverty level, or if she did, such
concern was not a serious obstacle in the effort to develop her
own literary voice.

ɕh ʀɕ

The process of writing offers the opportunity to surprise yourself at how well and how precisely you can use the language,
and how that precision leads to a natural voice and point of
view. The delight comes over time, as you write more, as you
build confidence, as you convince yourself that what you have to

say is entirely your thinking, and is clear and distinctive.

I see my editor's job as clearing away everything else. My task is suggested by the classic advice on how to sculpt an elephant: you get a chisel, a hammer, and a large block of granite; then you chip away everything that doesn't look like an elephant. Much of writing is a process of chipping away. It is sometimes chipping the cleverest lines, the funniest stories, so that the elephant you carve is like no one else's. A writer, like a sculptor, is satisfied only when there is nothing left but a precise, stylish, and singular expression.

This all may seem to you a daunting undertaking. We are barely into Chapter 2 and I already have you sculpting enormous mammals. But do not be intimidated.

Writing is not, for example, like the game of golf, where your teacher wears an entirely straight face as he offers 97 Critical Thoughts to Remember and Apply During Your Swing. You must keep your left arm rigid, your knees bent, your eye on the ball, your toes slightly flexed, your weight on the right side of the body until you shift it to the left side, your hands gripping the club loosely but not too loosely, your club speed not too fast, your attack on the back of the ball if it is a tee shot and on the bottom of the sphere if it is a wedge, and your mind on absolutely nothing at all, and above all you must relax, Relax, RELAX!—just to ensure that you do not deposit your ball in the nearby pond, which is inevitable anyway.

Writing does not require that you think a thousand thoughts at once. Writing is a natural process. In *The Complete Book of Running*, Jim Fixx suggested that running—eventually—is spiritually rewarding because it connects us to our ancestors, to a basic behavior in our lives. Writing is similarly rewarding and basic; it is a form of communication that is simple, direct, satisfying—and universal.

There is a delight in the community of language. Once you decide to become a writer you begin to notice more than ever before how writers have created miracles with mere words. You appreciate sounds, rhythms, and the images that language can suggest. You pay attention to the way others speak and to the way others write. When you reintroduce yourself to *Huckleberry*

Finn you take special note of Huck's lament aboard the Mississippi raft, when all activity stops because he has become "powerful lazy." You think about that combination of two words that customarily do not go together, and of the wry and delicious possibilities of language. You understand that you must overcome the natural condition of powerful laziness when it comes to writing.

Here's another way to make your own powerful lazy example. You go to the grocery store and arrive at the checkout counter with the following in your cart: celery hearts, frozen angel hair pasta, a bottle of pimientos, Dijon mustard, scouring pads, strawberry yogurt, Raisin Bran, eight garlic bagels, two packages of turkey sausage, and a can of liver cat food. Nothing highly unusual, nothing newsworthy. Yet as common a behavior as grocery shopping is—everyone does it—it is likely that never before in shopping history has this particular and precise collection of goods been assembled in one cart. It is also true that this collection is uniquely yours—it reflects your own personal view of nutritional and budgetary values. That is, although you use a common behavior, you nevertheless demonstrate unique expression.

Collections of words, of course, offer much greater rewards than turkey sausage and accompaniments. And once you begin to think of the possibilities—of the ways to say precisely what you mean when you fill your literary cart with personal and carefully chosen items—you have a much better opportunity for effective expression.

This is not to reduce writing to a trip through the aisles, only to serve as metaphor. We all share a common language, and some common wisdom, but we each have a unique view of life, and we are each capable of choosing a grocery cart of foods or a paragraph of words that makes a singular statement.

What you do with that cart is another issue. You must look at each writing opportunity—even if it promises to lead you to greater things—as your last. That is, you must express yourself fully and effectively on the subject you have chosen.

Writing requires that you become willing to stand up for what you think. It requires that you put aside any notion of worrying about reaction to your opinions. You have become a writer because you have something to say to people. Otherwise why write? You must trust in the written word—your written word.

Sometimes it takes much of a lifetime to come to that realization, even when there are signs aplenty that a person demonstrates much ability.

Nancy Slonim Aronie's first writing instinct occurred in the third grade when she wrote a birthday card to her mother. It said, "Happy birthday to Mom, to Mom, from Nancy and Tom." Her mother thanked her and said it was a fine card, but then asked, "Who's Tom?" "There is no Tom," Nancy replied. She knew right then there didn't have to be a Tom.

In high school she read J. D. Salinger, and a certain intimidation factor disappeared. "Salinger spoke my language," she recalls. "For the first time I didn't have to write 'whilst' or 'cometh.' I could actually say what was in my heart. My English teacher read my stuff out loud to the class. He would say, 'This is what I'm talking about' when trying to make a point about good writing. But I still didn't think of writing as a gift—or as important. I wrote too easily, too fast, never changed anything, never polished. My high school journalism teacher would ask for a piece for the school newspaper and I dashed it off. I thought the assignment had nothing to do with my worth. She was only asking me because my desk was close to hers. Then I won a gold key from Senior Scholastics for essay writing. I thought it was because they needed to give it to *someone*. I never thought of myself as a writer, or that what I wrote was special.

"My uncle, now there was someone special. He worked for Associated Press and wrote crime stories for *Official Detective* magazine. I finally wrote to him and said I wanted to be a writer. He wrote back, 'Girls don't write.' Oh, OK. I accepted that. I had never seen a woman newspaper reporter. There was no defiance. OK, I'll be a teacher. I never thought, hey, the hell with him.

"I didn't think in terms of writing being in my blood. My

father wrote a lot, on the back of envelopes, constantly writing little Ogden Nash-type things to my mother. He also didn't value his writing. He was a real model for 'This doesn't really count.' I did the same thing—I lost the scraps of paper I wrote on.

"Then, when college came, I whipped off this and whipped off that. I became class historian. I was known as a writer, but not to myself. I was a drama major. I was in productions. I wrote a play. I wrote for the newspaper, and for the literary magazine. Again, I didn't save anything.

"Then I got married and had babies and was absolutely miserable. I didn't do anything creative. It hit me one night when we went to an artist's opening. The woman was making animated films. At that time in my life I was shopping for Marimekko fabric, and getting my matched bowls, and having people for dinner, and wondering what to wear. That night I got home and fell across the bed and sobbed and said to my husband, Joel, 'What am I doing with my life?' and Joel said, 'What's the matter?'

"Some time later, it occurred to me that I could be a writer *and* a mother. I started writing poetry, and I went to readings and I knew my stuff was better than what I was hearing. And then I thought, how long am I going to sit here and say that? I started doing readings. People would laugh out loud at my humor, and I knew I was doing something right. But still I had no respect for it. I was just doing it so I could breathe.

"One January, I went to Martha's Vineyard alone—Joel had the kids, and I had a nourishing month. I had tea, I wrote, I wrote some more. I sent a story off to *Dark Horse Review*, and the phone woke me—they would pay $200, and I screamed into the phone. Someone who didn't know me was actually going to pay me for my writing! It had nothing to do with, 'Oh, she's just a nut.' I was the person people loved being around because I was the far-outness for them. I was their nut case. I would write, and they would say, 'Well, you know Nance.' Now, somebody who was a perfect stranger, somebody who had no idea about the nut case, thought my writing was worthy."

Nancy began submitting to *Northeast*. She sent a story called

"The Doppler Effect." I could not tell from reading it whether it was fiction or nonfiction. All I knew was that I adored it; the story explored the relationship of a husband and wife with detail and insight. I called Nancy and introduced myself, and did not ask if the piece was fiction. I simply said, "Where did the story come from?"

She told me that much of it was rooted in truth, and then proceeded to tell me things that later shocked her. Why did she tell a stranger about her own marriage? she wondered.

"But that positive reaction to the piece was really the beginning for me," she says. "Here I was in a big magazine, with hundreds of thousands of readers. It was gorgeously presented. I felt treated like a real writer. I said to myself, 'Hey, you're a writer.' "

Nancy then sent an essay about teaching children the meaning of death. Recalling our meeting later, for purposes of this book, she said, "When we sat down at lunch, you had the piece all circled. You said, 'This part is garbage, this part is shit, and this is gold—this is your voice—and you circled it. 'This is really you. Leave this other stuff out. This is what other people write.'

"I had just been trying to fill it up to make words. I was quoting other people. I was trying to show death—an important subject—so I looked it up in the anthologies. I was pulling stuff from the 'pros.' It was so obviously puzzle-pieced together, and not from my heart. You said to me, 'Nobody can say it better than you. Be true to your view.' "

Nancy got a tremendous response to that essay and others in the magazine and even then had a fragile outlook. She put together a tape to submit to "All Things Considered," the news program on National Public Radio. "At the time, they had not run commentaries, but I got an immediate response. They said they loved my stuff, and would I do them biweekly? I was so fragile that when they said five minutes was too long, I took it as a rejection. Then *Rolling Stone* called in response to a story I sent. They said they didn't do fiction but they loved the piece. I thought it was a rejection. *Esquire* said it was a woman's story, and could I make it a man's story? I took that as a rejection."

It wasn't, of course. But writers crave constant reinforcement that their work is acceptable, particularly at the beginning of their careers. Once Nancy knew that editors not only tolerated her but sought her, she relaxed, she became herself. She wrote naturally. Here are excerpts from a piece in which she masterfully wove commentary about her mother (Henny) and herself in the guise of the simple accounting of a trip to Martha's Vineyard and a match of Scruples, a game that tests each player's morality:

There were two Beas, a Sara, and a Henny. All in their seventies, all silver-haired senior citizens, two widows, two with husbands in my driveway waving their forlorn "What am I going to do about dinner tonight?" good-byes.

Five of us off to the Vineyard. For bridge, for quiet, for adventure. And I am the tour guide. It is my promise to my mother for her seventy-third birthday. The priorities are pills, pillows, and peppers. Pills for high blood pressure, pillows for sitting, for propping a broken wrist and cushioning an old disc operation, and peppers—Henny can't eat 'em. Sara doesn't eat any dairy; one Bea doesn't like greasy; the other doesn't eat spicy. . . .

We played Scruples.

The food in the restaurant is a total rip-off but the harried waitress does her best to provide good service. Do you leave her a tip?

"Of course," says Bea number one.

You're a high school principal. Do you hire a competent teacher who is a homosexual?

"Of course," says Sara.

In the supermarket you send a dozen packages tumbling into the aisle. No one sees you. Do you walk away?

"Of course," says Henny.

This is a game of honesty. This is a generation I never thought of as particularly honest. With themselves, with each other. About feelings, things, philosophies, emotions. And yet these women, who have been friends for sixty years, hide nothing.

You are at a dinner party and hear a distinct crack as a corpulent guest settles into an antique chair. The hostess is in the kitchen. Will you tell her what happened?

"Yes. No. Depends." Bea says. "Depends on what?" we demand. "It depends on who my friend is: the hostess or the fat behind."

You are waiting at a red light at 4:00 A.M. There isn't a car in sight. Do you go through the red light?

"Who is driving around at four o'clock in the morning?" Sara asks.

"That's not the question, Sara. Would you?"

"Depends," Sara says. We decide "depends" is a cop-out. We eliminate it. We are left with yes and no.

They asked me over blackened bluefish and arugula salad what I fear most about reaching their age. I find myself crying. Maybe it's the pillows, maybe it's the pills. Maybe it's that I don't want to stop riding my bike. I don't want to hurt in the morning in my knees. I don't want brittle bones. . . . "I guess I don't want to lose husbands and kids and stuff," dabbing my eyes and swallowing my sun-dried tomatoes.

I ask them what they miss about being my age. Having your energy and losing our dreams, they answer. By the time you're seventy, they say, you probably won't realize a lot of what you thought you would. That's hard, they agree. We talk about opportunities lost, choices not made, affairs not had, risks not taken. Would they trade places with anyone else?

Bring back Depends. . . .

In that short space, Nancy used humor and vivid description juxtaposed against serious thought (losing children and swallowing sun-dried tomatoes). She was willing to expose raw thoughts—her own raw thoughts, a thing necessary to make her piece believable, for a writer must establish a one-on-one relationship with the reader. There is only one way to do that: trust between the two. In Nancy's writing there is inherent trust, because long ago—in that piece about death—she discarded the extraneous, the thoughts that weren't hers that appeared only for effect. There is now no posturing, no holier-than-thou attitude, no phoniness.

Nancy's courageous words were in sharp contrast to her fragile confidence. It took years before she changed her mind about her talent. It took innumerable *Northeast* appearances. It took reprints in magazines around the country. It took "All Things Considered" commentaries, feature articles and columns for *Lear's*, establishing her own writing school, and collaborating on a musical comedy before she permitted herself to call herself a writer—before she gave herself permission to spend most of her day at the word processor and not feel guilty that it was "only writing."

The Private I

"Voice Lessons" and Thoughts on Approaching the Starting Lines

---

Where does a writing career begin? There is no ordained place. Certainly Jean Gonick would never have come across a writing text that instructed, "Wait until you're thirty-three years old and depressed because your gentleman friend has just dumped you after four years, leaving you even more miserable than before, considering you've spent your work days in a comatose fashion as a stupid administrative assistant and you haven't written a word in your boring adult life except in personal letters. Then after watching the movie *Picnic* at your girlfriend's apartment, sit down at her typewriter and, in your hypnotic state, record what happened and how you feel about it. That night, without thinking of the consequences or just how many thousands of readers you'll be letting into your most private thoughts, insert the pages in an envelope and send it off to the local magazine editor who you heard didn't mind reading the work of unknowns."

No, these instructions would never appear anywhere. No writing book can anticipate, or ought to anticipate, the particulars of a writer's experience or emotional makeup. The best it can do is instruct the writer or would-be writer that all experiences, positive or not, feed the mental reservoir that eventually may flow into serious writing.

For Jean Gonick, the emergence was not eventual. It burst out of her. There she was at her friend's place, tired, confused or, as she puts it, "insane" over the collapse of her personal and professional life. When the movie was over, Jean sprang to the borrowed typewriter to pour it out. "I was operating from a totally unconscious place. I was not thinking about what I was doing. It was some basic survival instinct. I was truly in emotional bad straits. This was my outlet."

The breakup of her relationship was documented in an essay in which milestones were the dinners she and her boyfriend had shared. Her symbol for the good times was the passionately prepared entree for which she, out of necessity and interest, was the producer. To mark the drifting and decline of the relationship, she described the era of the carryout barbecued chicken.

"It was one thing to write it," she says, "it was another to mail it as I did almost immediately. That was the leap of faith. That I would try to publish it is something I would not have anticipated. Here I was, just floating and emoting, and offering it up for everyone to see."

In "Cuisine of a Failed Romance," Jean documented the seasons. Like Vivaldi, she began in spring:

> The first time I had him to dinner it was important that everything be fresh, innovative, spontaneous and lovely. I chose linguine and fresh clams. I gambled on the prospect that he would love fish, relish the ritual of detaching the clams from their possessive shells and admire the tenderness of fresh pasta. It worked. He was impressed. It was an edible love project—not without design, certainly, but it comforted and seduced.

Jean's structure was simple, honest, and easily digestible. The reader sensed, of course, that if you begin with spring you necessarily end in the coldness of winter:

> We parted ways, sadly, stupidly, in all the confused defeat in which such separations are made. I am looking upon the vista of single-unit cooking again.
> I have done it before and know how it works: many artichokes and game hens, and muffins with unhappy toppings. . . .

Unhappy toppings, led, however, to happy professional endings. The first editor who published her told her about the reprint industry, and that if she wasn't prudent about mailing off her personal life it might be spread for all to read in distant magazines in Cleveland, Miami, Detroit, and Philadelphia. And so it happened. Sunday magazines around the nation began reprinting her work. Within two years Jean Gonick—or, more precisely, Jean Gonick's life and loves—became a hot national story. "I found out I could write one story and have it appear ten times, and get paid each time. It was amazing how often I got published."

Good writing tends to find its market. It gets noticed. The word quickly spreads. A writer who thinks that personal complications could not possibly be of interest to anyone else is thinking the wrong way. The person across the hall was interested in Jean's news, as was the person across town, as was, it turned out, the person across the nation. And the writing exercise inspired by a distressing moment in her life eventually ended with that distressing moment—and a few other more upbeat episodes from a life—in a book published by Random House entitled *Mostly True Confessions: Looking for Love in the Eighties.*

Moments such as the one that Jean described are very often the starting point in writing lives. From there, these writers eventually must digress from the narrow confines of events in their own lives to reporting on the lives of others through a perspective developed and enhanced by such literary and emotional training.

Jean is now offered regular assignments for *Mademoiselle, GQ, Self, Savvy,* and *Cosmopolitan.* Her work tends to be less often about her own life and more about the lives of others as seen by a perceptive writer who has experienced no shortage of emotion. She says, "In terms of subject matter, now I get to explore the terrain of other couples trying to make their hideous relationships work—which is much more fertile ground."

This has been, for Jean Gonick, a relatively short struggle to find her confidence and her voice as a writer.

ॐ ॐ

If you have attended writing seminars or read magazines that promise keys to the literary kingdom—if indeed you have paid attention here—you have run across the phrase "writer's voice." Yet it remains an elusive concept, and even though words are the tools of their living, writers are customarily no better at explaining their voices than composers their music or artists their paintings. I recall one panel discussion devoted to the definition of and elaboration on voice. A prominent columnist, a writer of bestselling nonfiction books, and a variety of others who had achieved some renown all spoke at some length on the matter of voice, yet none could pinpoint exactly what was meant by it. They agreed only that voice is indispensable. One of the writers did make this observation: "Some of my readers, upon meeting me, say that I talk the way I write." Beyond that, they offered little help. The effect merely reinforced the audience's befuddlement and the idea that everything that goes on in the mind of the writer is mysterious and undocumentable. The effect was to suggest to prospective writers that they have to be in the "writer's club" to get this key, but they cannot get into the club without that key.

The key to a voice, however, is available to all, in the way it was available to Jean Gonick. That key is a letter on the top row of the typewriter—the ninth letter of the alphabet. It is the physical and metaphorical "I." All effective writing—whether in the first person, the second, or the third, whether essay, nonfiction narrative, profile, fiction, or poetry—has a common denominator: the strong presence of the writer. The craft of writing is really a lifelong pursuit of the formation, refinement, and application of the writer's point of view, collection of knowledge, and personal style—in short, the writer's voice.

As the key to Jean Gonick's success was entirely within her own "private I," that same key is entirely within you. The purpose of this volume is to teach you the ways to find and develop that voice, and to urge you not to underestimate its potential power. Remember this: No one else brings to a subject your particular set of experiences, knowledge, curiosity, passion, eye for detail, or viewpoint. Do not be discouraged that a subject has been written about by others; it is not possible for any writer to write it the way you would—that is, if your voice is really your own.

If, for example, Lila Beldock Cohen had put aside her thoughts on the decline of promising love because Jean Gonick had covered it adequately, she never would have written in the third-person voice this piece based on her own personal archive of events and perceptions. As you see, the subject and technique are very much related to Jean Gonick's, but the singularity of personal point of view is clearly revealed:

> It had seemed logical for them to marry. They shared the same intellectual interests: they rang doorbells for the same candidates, picketed for the same causes, wrote outraged letters to newspapers for the same outrages. They had met, in fact, at a party to raise funds for some cause. Neither could remember the cause, but they had shared wine and crackers and slightly rancid cheese dip, so it followed that they discussed the issues and he took her home. And then it was the Museum of Modern Art, and Carnegie Hall, and evenings in small bars where jazz was played and the wine was cheap and worldly. It came about that one bright day they went to a jewelry shop and he bought her a small, but tasteful, engagement ring: she bought him a gold Cross pen-and-pencil set to keep in the desk in the office where he had recently begun to practice law.
>
> They were so busy going from one doorbell to the next, one meeting to the next, one magazine subscription to another, that there was never time to discuss their own needs, their own fears. To the small apartment on the East Side they brought, each one, boxes and boxes of books and phonograph records, furniture made of light wood and woven reeds, thick coffee mugs, Mexican throw rugs, wind chimes; brought, each one, a hope chest filled only with darkness, and unseen shadows of their own lives. . . .

Lila, you may assume, goes on in her essay to record the decline of a relationship. But the tone is much different from Jean's. Lila's voice is darker and deeper and yet just as illuminating, expressing intense and telling detail. And yet, like Jean's, it connects manifestations of love with undeveloped emotions.

ꝏ ꝏ

If the "I" is the key to serious writing, the personal essay is often the route to developing the breadth and personality of that pronoun. I say this with the sort of trepidation reserved for any editor who for over twenty years has received thousands of essays that range anywhere from mediocre to hideous. To a very misleading degree, the personal essay may be the most inviting of forms to the novice writer who is certainly aware of the common advice, "Write what you know." Therefore, every September I am the largely unappreciative recipient of what dozens of people knew about their summer vacations; every Mother's Day I am bombarded by mawkish sentiment for a relative who, I am to surmise, goes without such regard for the remainder of the year; and at regular intervals in all seasons I am exposed to silly tributes to dogs, cats, and even budgies.

The "cute" essay, written more for effect than for revelation, is the sort of stuff that must have moved Truman Capote to distinguish between those who type and those who write. Yet I hesitate to mention criticism from on high of the best intentions of novices; it reinforces the idea of Us vs. Them, the Gifted vs. the Illiterate Masses. Be comforted to know that it isn't the fact of personal references that makes such writing fail. It is the insincerity, the lack of craft, the lack of honest reflection and truth.

For the real truth is that I have indeed published Mother's Day tributes, and pet pieces, and vacation humor, because some of them work. Some of them are written by people who, like Jean Gonick, speak honestly and stylishly to the page, who type the truth, even when it is sometimes painful. "Our Wonderful Vacation" comes to mind, a piece by John Rothchild that was rueful, ironic, and spoke volumes about husbands and wives whose expectations for their travels, and for each other, tend to exceed reality. The longer the trip, Rothchild argued, the higher the expectations, the deeper the disappointments, the more incumbent it is on the travelers upon their return to provide falsely positive accounts of such journeys. And when Joe Kirkup compared the life of his stray dog, Shep, to his own aimlessness, he turned out a moving portrait of two pals. Such pieces are written by those who understand that, in writing about the telling particulars of their lives, some of which may require revealing to strangers conclusions clearly unflattering, they may touch a universal chord. They touch off in readers a very high compliment that may not sound much like a compliment at all: "I could have written that." What they really mean is that a writer has succeeded in verifying a private emotion of the reader, has seduced the reader into sharing the joy of the community of language.

Consider, for example, the reaction to Bice Clemow's report on the consequences of turning eighty, in which the author had the gumption to document the decline of his own body. In "The Me Degeneration," he wrote:

The body is the most mysteriously magical instrument ever invented. Take memory: I can forget that I just brushed my teeth, yet remember, hardly without thinking, the name of the nice woman who clerked in Wm. Powers's men's store twenty years ago and now watches out after Russ Pfau in the hardware store. Young friends of mine (that's people sixty) complain about forgetting names, addresses and recipes, a confession presumed to make us dodders feel better about the degenerative disaster. Whoever called it The Golden Age wasn't in it. Better would be The Daze of the Open Fly. Kind friends whom I meet in the post office softly cup their hands at my ear with a reminder. I tell them about Winston Churchill's addressing the House of Lords without the final touch of dressing. A member sent up a note of sartorial alarm. Churchill glanced down at the note and said, "The Prime Minister thanks the gentleman member but reminds him that dead birds don't fall out of the nest." There is absolutely no way to put a nice face on the senility that sends you off to the library and back home without returning the books. Don't tell me it just

happens to all of us! I know I cleaned my teeth; the
brush is wet. . . .

Well, talk about vulnerability—every private part explored!
The universal chord, you see, is struck in the honest detail. It
is in the self-revelation. If you write an effective personal essay,
you will learn that you will say things on the page that you
might wish you did not have to say. What separates the dreadful
little essay from one that enriches lives is really a feeling based
on subjective guidelines: How natural is the writer's voice? How
real is the subject matter? Has the writer used the incident
described to interpret the chain of events, to draw conclusions
based on reporting and a rich perspective? Is the writer offering
something beyond the narrative to illuminate the subject for
readers who may face the same circumstance? Is the writer
risking something? Or is the writer's purpose merely to present
himself or herself in the best possible light (and therefore what
emerges seems fraudulent and gratuitous)?

If the answers to these questions are the correct ones, then
the universal chord will be struck. Here, for example, is one of
the dozens of letters from readers Bice received: "Thank you.
Expressed my eighty-two-year-old attitudes perfectly. Copies go
out to my five children, twenty-two grandchildren, even to my
thirteen great-grandchildren. They hopefully will get the mes-
sage. I have to decline weddings, birthdays, cookouts, and
dinner, shopping at the mall, trips to Ireland, Disney World. I
could go on."

And, as for Jean Gonick, she tells the story of sitting in a
restaurant overhearing a couple discussing a piece of Jean's that
had just appeared that morning, quoting the article, arguing
over its meaning and how it applied to their own relationship.
"Most people," she says, "never heard of me, but the columns I
write now are the basis for them to examine their own neuroses.
In that case, the couple said of the piece, 'Wasn't that good. But,
well, you can't be funny all the time.' It was just so astonishing
to be talked about for even one minute."

☙ ❧

In her instructive insider's view, *The Writing Life*, Annie Dillard counsels to "write as if you were dying. At the same time, assume you write for an audience consisting solely of terminal patients. That is, after all, the case. What would you be writing if you knew you would die soon? What could you say to a dying person that would not enrage by its triviality?"

Dillard's advice pertains to the serious state of mind and purpose required by those who intend to improve their writing. I presume here to take her notion figuratively and literally.

If I were forced to identify one subject that opens the door to serious writing it would be the subject of death. Odd how this end so often signals a beginning. Yet overwhelmingly it is the subject of choice for those who would pick up a pen for the first time. Writing about loss is a way to grieve, and a piece of writing paper is a fine place to explore deep feelings.

No less a writer and statesman than Vaclav Havel says, "Part of why most writers write is to divert their despair into their writing, and thereby overcome it."

Karen Devassy, a physician whose livelihood requires that she face death in a professional manner, often discussed these issues with survivors. But when she lost her own husband to cancer after twenty years of marriage, she found herself as unprepared as anyone she had ever counseled and comforted. For weeks she could not leave her house through the front door for fear of seeing the flower beds her late husband, Davis, had planted.

"I began to recover only when I realized I was allowing the flowers to control me," she says. "Depression is caused by lack of control. I knew I had to control the situation. I finally decided to walk out the front door—and to write about Davis. Once you can organize your thoughts, your thoughts don't control you anymore. I cried over the piece I wrote, but as I wrote it I could document my healing. Being creative, I found, is a great high. Thinking about sentences and words is a rewarding process."

Questions of death inspire expressions of life. Certainly this is a primary reason the subject is so pervasive. But another is that death necessarily removes that innocence of expression, the doubting that all writers and would-be writers have, the attitude expressed in the question, "What does it matter what I think?" Death makes us confront feelings.

Earlier I mentioned briefly the work of Joe Kirkup. For Joe the unspeakable death of Joe Knowl was the beginning of both a writing life and a healing process. I had read a response he sent to the *Miami Herald* editorial page concerning new research on Vietnam vets, and had called him because it seemed he might have much more to say. He came into the office reluctantly and said, "Listen, I'm no writer. I'm just a redneck drifter who's mad as hell about Vietnam. . . . I'm not like you intellectual softies. . . . I can't even type." I gave him four pads of legal paper and said, "Here, be back in a week with your Vietnam essay." He said, "All right. But it won't be what you expect." What Joe Kirkup wrote for *Tropic* magazine in 1978 was an extraordinary essay born out of anger, frustration, and, until then, unaddressed guilt over his own role in Vietnam. And, although the writer likely would not have admitted it, it was an essay that revealed great love. It began:

> I heard a really sad bit of news . . . that half as many Vietnam vets have committed suicide as were killed in the war. It means that many thousands of us couldn't get used to being blind, or couldn't rationalize our paraplegia, or just never learned to live with the ghosts. . . .
>
> I am a lucky one. Every morning . . . I take a few silent moments to appreciate that I can see and walk and hug my old mongrel with both arms. All I have to deal with is the ghosts. . . .
>
> Some of the ghosts have names. Joe Knowl was a sandy-haired, bright-eyed hell-raiser from Rhode Island. His wife had a baby while we were on the troop ship to 'Nam. I guess the kid is about 14 now, the same age as her father's ghost. . . .
>
> "A" company was stopped on a dirt road in the Michelin rubber plantation, west of Saigon. We were looking up at the road as a group of Viet Cong crossed it about 800 meters away. There was no way to catch the VC on foot, so the responsibility for taking their lives fell upon the awesome artillery power at my command. I took out my map and quickly estimated the coordinates of the enemy unit. Within a minute I had initiated a fire

mission from a battery of huge 144-millimeter howitzers about 10,000 meters away.

The first volley exploded on the road where the VC had crossed, the second hit about 400 meters closer to us, and the third ripped the heart right out of "A" company's forward platoon and right out of Joe Knowl's chest.

I called for a cease-fire and scrambled toward the front of the unit amid the screams and the smoke and the broken rubber trees.

We found Knowl on the ground on his side like a dog that had been hit by a truck. He was covered in white powder and dust. There was a huge hole through the center of his chest from one side to the other. The shrapnel had smashed his rifle and carried parts of it into his body. . . .

I looked down at his face, a face that had always worn a smile. His eyes and ears were leaking blood and his upper teeth protruded over his lower lip as death had taken him in the midst of agony.

I have seen that face at least once a day for 14 years. I have seen his broken body in dreams where the face was replaced by those of friends and family. I have wished a thousand times that I hadn't called for that artillery, or that the gunners hadn't been so stoned that they failed to re-check their sights. I wish that Joe Knowl were alive, but he's not. He's only a ghost, my ghost. . . .

This piece was picked up by magazines across the country and spurred a flurry of other work that was just as enthusiastically received by various editors and reading audiences. Obviously Joe was able to channel his anger and frustration in a positive direction.

Why is it that death—or death-related subjects—bring out new expressions? It is the time in our lives when we strip away all that's superficial, when we are reduced to our most basic feelings, when we have the greatest capacity for honesty. And it is that honesty that is at the core of good writing.

I confess I did not think I would tap into such honest feelings when I wrote to Katharine Hepburn in December 1981. This native of Hartford was certainly an obvious subject for my magazine, but I was not interested in just another profile, particularly in that she was notorious for not giving writers much beyond the time of day and a tour through her gardens. I had the idea that a woman of such rich expression might someday want to take a profile into her own hands; that after seventy-four years she would put the story straight herself in a magazine-length memoir. My entreaty at first brought only this reply: "Dear Lary Bloom: If I can think of something. Katharine."

The "something" occurred a few weeks later. She landed in Hartford Hospital, where her father long ago had worked as a surgeon, suffering injuries from an automobile accident. News reports indicated that her left leg was so badly damaged that amputation was considered. But they did not indicate Miss Hepburn's confrontation with mortality. She saved that for her ultimate response to my letter—her recollections of childhood and thoughts of returning to those same grounds. The piece opened a new kind of communication for her, one that led eventually to her autobiography. In "My Hometown" she wrote:

> . . . My goodness—now that's a funny thing. Here I am again in Hartford. Where I came from. Where I'll come to die. Well, no, no—don't cringe. That's not dreary. I mean that's practical. That's inevitable, isn't it? You have a place where you're born and you go off and you become whatever you become. Then there will come a time—well, the "wandering on" time. You know what I mean. And it's nice if maybe you're sick or not quite up to it, to have a place to come back to—your real home—where there's even a piece of ground waiting for you. And your own dear ones. A place where you know the gravestones and the trees and the flowers and you'll go in that old gate on Fairfield Avenue and—but actually I'm ahead of myself. At least I think I am. I hope.

That she was a household name certainly helped the piece, but honest emotion is of universal appeal, no matter the status of the writer. She wrote neither up nor down but directly to the reader. She was in command of her subject matter. She was even in command of her punctuation, a matter that consumed nearly two days of negotiation, in which I argued without great success against the proliferation of dashes. And yet, looking back, all those dashes were her: they reflected her urgencies, her determination, her voice. And, most of all, this piece allowed her to reveal something significant—and very private—on a subject that she had honored with lifelong silence.

One other point, aside from the punctuation, that may seem obvious: you could sense her working the thoughts out on the page. If we accept the idea that a writer writes for the same reason a painter paints or a composer composes—it is the chosen form of communication, the best for that person—it must also be true that it is in the writing that the best thinking comes out. You as a writer need not necessarily know all you want to say about a particular subject, only that you know that in the writing itself a significant and singular point of view may very well emerge.

ᴐʰ ᴄʲᴇ

These pieces, of course, had mortality as a central theme. But remember Annie Dillard's urging. Death can be merely metaphorical—the image that allows entry into meaningful communication. The point is not that you should be so unfortunate as to forever interpret death for your readers, but that you should write as if you are writing the last piece you will ever write about your chosen subject. Or the last piece you will ever write at all. You should write as if nothing else matters, especially not the consequences of your writing.

Sometimes it takes much courage, and it takes a commodity of which writers have an innate abundance, even if they don't always show it. That is, writers by their nature are insecure. That sense of vulnerability, as it applies to pieces they are writing, is crucial to the connection with readers. No personal piece, that is, no serious personal piece, can be effective unless the writer is at least aware that reaction may make life uncomfortable.

Micki Savin's debut as an essayist—made in her sixties—

would not be without consequence. Her only published piece to that point was a few paragraphs she had sold for twenty-five dollars to a newspaper travel section. But, like many mature people, Micki was at a point at which honest and full expression was a very appealing prospect. She wanted to go well beyond the far ends of the earth, where she commonly explored, into the most mysterious of all places, her deepest feelings. She might have done so in private. It would have saved her the negative reaction from people who she had considered friends. But it also would have prevented her from making the connection it did to many grateful strangers.

As background, you should know that Hartford is a starchy, stoic town—it is a town, people like to say, that was built on the absence of risk; this is because of its prominent insurance presence. In such a setting it is not incumbent upon respectable members of society to express emotion. Or even, it seems, to admit having emotion. So when Micki decided to write a piece about her search for a male companion, she was in a sense breaking new social ground in a very conservative place. She told how, after two years of mourning her late husband, Isador, she felt lonely. Her piece told of the personals ad she placed in what she thought would be a suitable journal, the *New York Review of Books*.

The consequences of the article were real enough. Neither her initial search nor the response to the *Northeast* article led to a satisfying relationship. And the article itself shocked her long-time acquaintances. How could she do such a thing? How could she say the things she said in public? How at her age could she crave what she was apparently craving? Which is precisely the reason the piece was so popular, so telling—so universal—it demonstrated that no age is too advanced for tenderness and affection. There was a very positive response among people she hadn't known; they found in her candid report feelings they had felt but had left unexpressed. In that state, feelings bottled inside, readers often consider themselves oddballs. When a thoughtful, courageous writer touches an emotion that a reader shares, a connection is made. The writing may help the writer as well. Micki says that, in writing this piece, "It was the first time

I wasn't my husband's wife. I wasn't somebody else. I was me."

If Micki Savin took on her horrified friends in the Hartford community, Ellen Stratton was more ambitious: she challenged an entire religion, or so it seemed.

Ellen began her writing career at the urging of writer/surgeon Richard Selzer, who called one day to advise me of a new and very special talent, a woman he had first met on the operating table. Resulting from that call were an essay on varicose veins and a series of superb, loosely autobiographical short stories. In the course of our conversations over the years, Ellen often made comments about her education, in particular her four years at Albertus Magnus College, which she had always referred to as Dogmatica College for Women. Such constant references led me to believe—as I tend to believe in such cases—that there was a piece there somewhere, and the occasion of the twenty-fifth reunion of her class was just the proper excuse. We anticipated, and we got, an uproar in reaction to the piece, an unflattering portrait of an education. This, even though in the very first paragraph Ellen had done her best to disarm her readers, to say right off that she was certainly not Holier Than Thou or Anybody:

> In 1963 I graduated from Albertus Magnus College in New Haven, a small Catholic liberal arts college for women. I graduated convicted of various crimes against the image of Albertus Womanhood, my daughter Alison as yet unborn, concealed nicely by my academic gown. Had the authorities known about Alison, we both would have been yanked straight to hell by my ankles, bypassing other penances I knew so well.

If the school was not heaven, the writer obviously was no angel. Her bold admission in the beginning of the piece indicated to the reader that honesty, not self-aggrandizement, would be the product of her pen. Yet as much as this trait of honesty is to be admired, it is not so admired that it will ward off passionate criticism by defenders of the faith, or equally passionate concerns about the editor, expressed by a newspaper publisher

who argued that publishing point-of-view pieces was an excellent idea as long as he agreed with the point of view. In short,
real writing is no place for the faint of heart.

ॐ ॐ

Well, here you are, buried in the third chapter, worried that no
extraordinary circumstance has occurred in your life—you have
not taken on the church, or placed personal ads, or returned
from Vietnam with great guilt, or were not left in the kitchen
alone facing the prospect of unhappy toppings—therefore you
will never capture the attention of the editor.

These examples are simply to show that it was serious subjects that enticed these writers to first express themselves on
paper in a serious manner. In every case, essays and pieces
followed that in terms of subject matter, approach, and tone
were much different. No longer was it required that the writer
draw only from experience.

And yet you must start somewhere, and you start inevitably
with what you know, even if, as we have said here, what you
know is merely the basis for a piece.

But, then, do you do it only at the urging of some editor? Must
you purchase a word processor to begin? Of course not. As you
progress in the business of writing, and as you begin to make a
living at it, you will purchase equipment and forge close relationships with editors. But if you don't know an editor, and have
enjoyed no encouragement from one, it doesn't mean that you
shouldn't write.

I had never met the senior citizen who so many years ago
wrote an angry open letter to the city of Akron about its failure
to protect its old people against young hooligans. But I proudly
published her piece. And, after fifteen years of publishing her
work, I still have never met Martha Munzer, now in her nineties,
who sent a piece to my slush pile that documented the extraordinary love between Martha and Isaac Corkland, whom she had
first met at age eighteen and finally married sixty years later.
Nor had I met "Homeless Joe" Moton until after he had written
his story in a spiral notebook (a story, by the way, that *Catholic
Digest* decided to reprint).

As for technique, it is true that in almost every venture neatness counts. And yet the more intent the editor is on finding quality material, the less concerned he or she is with justified right-hand margins. There have been any number of good pieces that have been written on notebook paper, and many of those were in the form of diaries or letters.

The letter approach is almost always successful with the beginning writer, who tends to be intimidated by both the project and the marketplace. "Will what I have to say seem important enough, or good enough?" This question can sometimes lead to heavy, turgid prose, with the real story buried where no impatient editor will find it. I usually suggest that the beginning writer (or, in many cases, the experienced reporter who has never written with a strong point of view) simply select a good friend and write a letter to that person telling the story. First, this approach defines the audience. That is, all good writing seems to speak directly to the reader. The beginning writer has no problem speaking directly to a friend, and the tone generally will be suitable for a large audience. In writing to a friend, the writer will not be self-conscious and will tell the story more naturally, which is, after all, the point. In addition, in such a communication with someone who cares about the writer there is more opportunity for candor. That is, it appears that the writing will be read by only one person, a person who cares about the writer's welfare.

This technique has worked dozens of times with new writers. Not long ago I asked a lawyer who had just been released from jail for cocaine possession to write about his addiction. He sat in my office on Friday night, a quizzical look on his face, wondering what he could write about, saying that it was unlikely he could document the sort of personal piece I had in mind. Not that he didn't want to—he just didn't know how. When I explained the letter approach, he said he would try. The following Monday morning—less than seventy-two hours later—he turned in a twelve-thousand-word letter to his cousin Stanley that was both a compelling narrative of his addiction and a revealing commentary on drugs in our society. I deleted the salutation and closing and had the basis for a very strong piece.

It is that natural story telling, that self-revelation, that touches both readers and editors. And it does not have to be about life-threatening issues.

Consider the case of J. J. Holcolm, whose little essay of life in the aisles of the grocery store, the first piece he ever wrote, earned him $250.

The real point is, however, that J. J. Holcolm didn't know he was writing an essay when he responded to a piece of mine about grocery shopping. He was writing a letter to the editor on notebook paper. It was such an astonishing look inside a big store and so brimming with good humor that I decided it should not be published as a letter. It deserved a page of its own.

And so J. J. Holcolm received the call, and heard the question writers are dying to hear: "What's your Social Security number?" It was then we learned that J.J., a genuine Hartford wit, had never made it past the eleventh grade.

But more than that, when he was in school, he had serious problems with writing; it was one of his weakest subjects. He always wrote awkwardly and ineffectively in the manner that teachers had insisted on. It was only years later, when he took pencil in hand and scribbled unself-consciously, thinking he was only writing a letter to the editor, that the real, passionate, persuasive expression—the natural voice—of J. J. Holcolm emerged.

4

The Point Is . . .

Considerations of the Writer as Seducer

The more you write, the easier it may become to perform a literary song and dance. On good days all your verbs will be active, all your participles undangling, all your metaphors apt. Even so, the yield of such technical wizardry may prove unsatisfying. As a writer you must acquire depth and authority. You must present a persuasive point of view.

To newspaper reporters, even some who have come to me in the hopes of widening their literary horizons, "point of view" is a foreign phrase. "What does it matter what I think?" is the question reporters inevitably ask. In their profession, objectivity is the most cherished standard. And yet objectivity is no obstacle to good writing. The real obstacle is a writer's mental detachment—the attitude that a writer is merely an observer, not a commentator. It is odd, but these same reporters who wonder at their involvement in the subject matter are the very ones who most appreciate Joan Didion's evocative case studies of community life, or Tom Wolfe's delicious derisions of the high and mighty, or Roger Angell's understated appreciation of the subtle human dynamics of baseball.

This is point-of-view writing in its highest form, and yet, when you examine its essence, you will see it relies on objective standards, primarily good reporting. But it uses such reporting as a basis, not as its ultimate end. No series of events is self-explanatory. We need writers to tell the stories of our lives in a

41

revealing way, to set us straight, to make sense of things, to touch us, to make us think. The way to do this is through the various avenues of point of view.

It may be helpful early to distinguish between mere opinion and point of view. The classic newspaper op-ed piece tends to be opinion; that is, a short recap of recent news with the author's spin on the events. Point-of-view writing is a broader and deeper technique in which opinion is but one characteristic. It relies on a writer's interpretation of the subject matter and is built upon a structure designed to tell a story effectively and allow the most persuasive argument. Having done original reporting (which op-ed pieces do not usually require), having made sense of the matters at hand, the writer acquires the authority to explain what happened and why without regard to public or institutional expectations. This technique is often nothing more complicated than an informed and critical telling of events, or a narrative, in which commentary is woven. Point-of-view writing, as you will see, is not so much a matter of blatant argument as it is literary seduction.

When the Connecticut General Assembly passed without much debate or delay the country's most liberal abortion law, the news pages of the *Hartford Courant* dutifully recounted details of the voting and the specifics of the law—with reaction, all of it predictably extreme, from the two sides. But the larger, unreported issue was one that did not escape writer Joel Lang, who initially questioned how, after years of public debate, some of it violent, the legislature could adopt an abortion bill so quickly. He also wondered how society's most divisive question so quickly could become a political nonissue. Such questions typically are not the subject of "facts." No news source, to that time, had even raised these issues. Yet Joel sensed that lurking behind the headlines were questions that might intrigue readers. They certainly intrigued him; and in such a case a writer's instinct is not to be ignored.

Answering these questions required dozens of interviews and many weeks. And even then there was still the key challenge: how to make sense out of what he found. The more he uncovered the parts of the political puzzle, the more these parts fit

together in his own mind. No single interview told everything.
But pieced together these interviews allowed Joel to reconstruct
the forces behind the vote, and in the process his point of view
revealed an illuminating interpretation of the legislative process.
Here, for example, is how he described how the legislature
settled on the name of the bill.

> Some suggested it be called "An Act Concerning Coun-
> seling," because a subsection required counseling for
> girls under 16. But it was feared the title would arouse
> the abortion-rights camp, which is wary of any obstacle
> to abortion. Similarly, "An Act Concerning Abortion"
> was rejected as a red flag to abortion opponents. The
> committee finally chose a title so neutral as to be mean-
> ingless.
>   The bill, which will affect thousands of people in the
> most intimate way, was called "An Act Concerning the
> Repeal of Certain Statutes."

In issuing opinions in op-ed pieces, or letters to the editor, or
in the original newspaper reporting, it is unlikely that the name
of this bill would even be mentioned. It would be considered
mere boilerplate. But in interpreting the legislative process Joel
showed the relationship of boilerplate and boiling point. Such
irony could be uncovered only because the writer took it upon
himself to learn what happened, digest the voluminous mate-
rials, and form them into an overall point of view.

As suitable a word as *interpretation* is to define point-of-view
writing, it is not enough. There is also the matter of passion. In
any writing project, there are moments when passion escapes
the writer, when the writer is at odds with the material, when
the point is lost, when the project seems too confusing or
uninteresting or impossible. The writer must then return to his
or her initial reasons for writing the piece and the need for
personal expression.

If there is one moment in the writer's mind that is most
telling, it is the moment that the instinct for the piece occurs.
You must remind yourself that persuasion, description, illumina-

tion, story telling, exploration of values are the reasons you write. Remind yourself that you have something important to say, and that the initial instinct, the key to your point of view, must be honored. This instinct is not, however, a convenient phenomenon. It does not appear only during working hours. It may pop up in the middle of a dinner party, at the ballpark, or in the shower. Do not dismiss these spontaneous moments. Write notes afterward, and read them the next day to see if the subject still interests you. If so, you have an excellent starting point. You need not be concerned that your point of view may be muddled; in the course of the work it will certainly develop.

Phyllis Rose is the author of several distinguished biographies, including those of Josephine Baker and Virginia Woolf. Her recent book of essays, *Never Say Goodbye*, is filled with evocative point-of-view pieces that started out merely as notions.

She told me that, "In writing those essays I never knew when I started where I was going to end up. Most of the fun for me in writing is that process of discovery. All I know at the start is that something interesting happened in my life, and that I ought to write about it." As to the event's significance, Phyllis subscribes to the old saw, "How do I know what I think until I see what I say?"

An example is a piece on teaching her son, Teddy, how to drive. "I thought what I had was a pedagogical problem—how to teach him." But as she wrote her narrative, describing that instruction process, it occurred to her that "the deeper problem was my own aging, and passing the torch to a new generation." Teaching Teddy to drive was a symbol that "I had served my biological function as a mother. And it made me angry." It also made for a rich narrative.

Early in this volume, reference was made to the emergence of such passion for writing and point of view in Sunday magazines. My own enlightenment was gradual. Yet if there was any one project that launched the independent attitude and passion that point-of-view reporting requires, it was a piece with a seemingly innocuous origin: the comics.

The spring of 1972 was still a raw time in Ohio when it came to the subject of Kent State. The country remained divided on Vietnam, and the tragic events at Kent two years earlier served only to polarize the issue even further. After student activists burned the ROTC building, Governor James Rhodes had activated the National Guard. The guardsmen proved unwilling to suffer insults and rocks in a confrontation in front of the communications building and began shooting. Nineteen students were wounded and four lay dead.

Kent State became a symbol of the protest movement. The rolling campus green where the blood had been spilled was a continuing battleground between those who supported the war and those who did not. Eventually commentary was to be found even in the comic pages, where an emerging new force, Garry Trudeau, marked the second anniversary of the shootings. In a series of strips, his "Doonesbury" characters commented on the events of May 4, 1970. One strip took up the issue of Attorney General John Mitchell's decision not to prosecute the guardsmen. That strip gave Zonker a chance to observe that May 4 had promised to be a very nice spring day in Kent, Ohio. In the last panel, Zonker, in a fit of sarcasm, wished John Mitchell "a very nice day."

Perry Morgan, then the editor of the *Beacon Journal,* had long been troubled by Trudeau. He had decided that "Doonesbury" was not really a comic strip but political commentary, and began to shuffle it about the paper, finally letting it rest in the classified section. When Morgan was alerted to the upcoming Kent State strips, he decided not to run four of them, including the John Mitchell episode. He pronounced them "not funny" and said that they only exacerbated the wounds of Kent State.

To James Ricci, a staff writer for *Beacon,* such an act was intolerable. There was no question this was censorship, a matter to be deplored and addressed. But how to address it? He worked for a magazine that was part of a newspaper that had banned the strips. Also, the magazine at that time was more a forum for the oddball report than for a meaningful issue. What happened over the next few weeks changed the course of his writing forever. "It was the first time I strove to be independent as a writer." And it certainly changed the course of *my* thinking and editing. From then on I thought outside the lines—outside the purview of the newspaper—but inside the provinces of point-of-view writing, of writing that matters.

Because our office was so cramped, and because the Sunday editor was not one to encourage free discussion before clamping down with his own version of censorship, Jim and I were obliged to talk over story ideas at a diner across the street. We must have returned with smirks on our faces that morning when the Sunday editor accused us of conspiracy. We denied the crime, but were certainly guilty. We had conspired to undertake a profile of Garry Trudeau and were about to ask the Sunday editor if he could lobby for the money to send Jim to Connecticut, where Trudeau lived. The Sunday editor's response was predictable: because the approval for travel had to come from the editor in chief, we didn't have a chance. "Ask anyway," we urged. "It's an important story. Our readers need to know what happened." We tried every argument we could think of, including thinly disguised flattery: "It would be a chance to show readers how open-minded we were about our close-minded attitudes." Such pleas were ineffectual at that level and had to be taken higher—to Perry Morgan himself, who surprisingly approved the travel funds.

Jim returned from a very fruitful trip and began writing. "It was a piece that was going to be wry, and sardonic, and something other than what I had written for the newspaper. And, being good children of the sixties, we were going to show we were not going to be intimidated by authority. So I decided to stick it to Perry Morgan right in the beginning." The profile began with a "conversation" between writer and subject in New Haven.

Have a lobster on Perry Morgan? Garry Trudeau said he'd just love to. After all, it was Morgan, wasn't it, who as editor of the *Beacon Journal* decided to excise Trudeau's

comic strip "Doonesbury" from the comic pages and
wrap it in disfavor and classified advertisements deep in
the bowels of the paper?

But, considerations of revenge aside, it has been a hard
day for Trudeau, renting a van and single-handedly
transferring all his possessions from an apartment to an
old, dank dormitory on Yale's campus.

Would Perry be willing to foot a couple of pitchers of
beer to go with the lobster? Sure he would. No matter the
fact that he wouldn't be there personally to pour. The
Old Heidelberg Restaurant, then. Fine, okay.

But we were not done when the piece was written. Jim and I
felt that, in order to present the issue intelligently, the four strips
that had been banned from the newspaper should be printed, so
readers could make up their own minds whether the newspaper
editor had acted judiciously. Predictably, the Sunday editor was
horrified. He said, "You'll have to get permission from Perry."

I found Perry Morgan emerging from a meeting of editorial
writers. He was a tall, quiet, gentlemanly man who took long
drags on his pipe before speaking. I summoned the gumption to
argue for printing the strips. I told Perry—and this guarantee is
always important in persuading a news source—that, although
the thrust of the piece might digress from his point of view, we
would certainly give him ample opportunity to express it in the
most effective way he could. That is, given the choice of a
hostile piece staring him in the face or one that would contain
to some degree his best thinking, he could clearly prefer the
latter.

Perry Morgan tilted his head down and looked over the top of
his glasses as he said only, "Do you have to?" I knew I had him.
I said, "Yes."

The project represented a great deal to us. It meant that there
were no boundaries when it came to subject matter or to responsible point of view. It meant, after a period of struggle and
search, that we finally understood our mission as magazine
journalists: to write what we thought without regard to consequence.

One of the most impressive pieces in the early days of *Beacon* was not one we had assigned ourselves, but one that arrived from the *Los Angeles Times* wire service, a remarkable piece of reporting and writing by Charles T. Powers. Powers documented the final hours in the career of a Firestone tire builder who was retiring after twenty-five years of service. I do not have a copy of that piece, but I certainly have kept the story in my mind. I could never forget Powers's distinct voice, his own view of what the workplace and the emptiness of retirement mean to the worker. I cannot forget his observation that it was the first day the worker ever had worn a suit to work; or that, in the gold-watch ceremony, the young supervisor had had to ask the foreman what the worker's name was; or that, assessing the five-minute retirement ceremony, Powers observed that "The gate to pasture swings on resonant hinges of ceremony" (just the sort of poetic vision and adult perspective that is the key to meaningful writing); or that the worker had been given the rest of the day off, and he had repaired to the local tavern without his buddies, and he had sat there on the bar stool, alone, with a gold watch on his wrist and time on his hands. Powers had written a feature story for the wires. But through his structure (following the worker closely that day, developing a narrative that built to an emotional climax), and through detail—describing the particulars of the day against the backdrop of the workplace in general—his point of view came across clearly and powerfully.

As Powers clearly demonstrated, being there is a distinct advantage for a writer; he did not rely on how others—those who do not make a living writing—saw this ceremony, but on how he himself had seen it. By choosing to tell the story in the framework of a day—weaving back to earlier times—Powers built a natural framework for the piece, one that easily engaged the reader.

This framework was one I employed many times over the years. When, for example, Stephen Jones told me that his favorite music store, Oliver's, was closing, I asked him to write about the last day as a way to speak about the long history of the place. This form was fruitful for Steve. "Blues for Oliver's" was eventually included in a volume of Steve's *Northeast* pieces published by W. W. Norton as *Short Voyages.* And he employed the same technique a couple of years later to describe another last day—another set of values.

He had shopped at Charlie Vincent's bookstore for twenty years. And now the proprietor was off to Maine to retire. Steve had browsed and bought many books there, books that the chains wouldn't think of carrying. These were volumes that piqued his curiosity, books about the sea. He told all that in the early part of the essay, and about Charlie himself. The last part of the essay featured this scene:

> When I came back the next day . . . the mood had changed. It was raining and Charlie stood in the door-way with his cigar's dampness competing with the weather. Contrary to what he'd indicated the day before, there were still a few items on the porch for sale, some ratty paperbacks about self-help, and foreign intrigue. There were also some non-literary objects, ashtrays and God knows. I picked up a couple of short brass curtain rods.
>
> "Could you do me a favor?" said Charlie. "Mind the store. Such as it is. I've got to run to the lawyer's."
>
> Inside the house, it seemed as damp as outside.
>
> And dark.
>
> There were no books or even shelving in the first room. I walked into the room that had held the wonderful maritime collection. There, where Conrad and Melville and Belloc and H. M. Tomlinson and Stevenson and Falconer had shone, was only the glare of a naked bulb. Where Drake and Magellan and Peter Freuchen and Frobisher and Slocum and Pidgon had sailed billowed four bulkheads of bilious wallpaper. At least I think it was wallpaper. I found myself pacing the room, my feet measuring the gritty carpet.
>
> Eight by eight.
>
> All that, my whole life, it seemed, once so expanded in this chamber. . . .
>
> Eight by eight.
>
> If that. . . .

Here is a passage worthy of those distinguished writers cited. It is full of description, insight, irony. If John Dryden was right—if the purpose of literature is to delight and instruct— Steve Jones's work is certainly a superb example of that school, even if "delight" is not the most precise way to describe the mood of the day. Notice how the writer wove literary references (references that were particularly significant to him) with a physical description of the store.

He could have said it more prosaically. He could have written, for example, "I found in that bookstore many volumes that affected me over the years written by Melville, Conrad, Stevenson, etc." But he chose to be metaphorical and understated. He used the vehicle of a bookstore's last hours to explore a point of view that contrasted his own limited physical world and boundless spiritual world.

There is much more to the art of Steve Jones. Yet the point of including him here is to learn how the writer's point of view— intimate and personal—speaks broader truths to the reader.

Certainly it requires the writer's honest view, and, as you see from the Charlie Vincent example, it does not do damage to the piece if there is a sense of irony, understatement, and rhythm. Or if the piece teaches us other things besides the writer's point of view. There were writers cited by Jones with whom I had not been acquainted. But notice that he did not mention them in a way meant to impress the reader with his voluminous knowledge of the literature of the sea. In fact, he did just the opposite. He praised Charlie Vincent, and in effect revealed the secret of how his own broad sea view had initially emerged from such a "limited" place. This is the sort of writing that touches readers and stays with them.

Steve's effectiveness, however, did not depend on charitable views. One of the pieces included in *Short Voyages* purported to be a commentary on the decline of the Christmas carol, but was, as you will read in only the first few paragraphs, a piece that used the subject matter—as in the Charlie Vincent piece—to explore values. That is, he both described and interpreted a series of events, and out of this came a point of view.

Walking into a store a week before Thanksgiving, I was

assaulted by Christmas music and, I'm afraid, fell to
cursing, whereupon I was challenged by the proprietor.
"What's the matter?" she said. "Don't you like Christmas
carols?"

"No," I said. "At least not . . ." and I waved my hand
toward the ubiquitous woofers and tweeters whence
issued the violins of Montovani.

A few evenings later as I reached for the TV button, I
heard a dismal cry from the street. Fumbling the curtains, I discovered an amalgam of what church groups
call "young people." They were intoning what could
have only been, by its lugubrious legato, the Franz
Gruber tune about the night's being silent.

Their eyes were not, however, after the manner of
Christmas card figures, uplifted piously, but rather
roamed furtively on what appeared to be mimeographed
copies of the words. There was even one tall goop who
held a flashlight which he cast about on the various
scripts like a meter man in a strange cellar. As for the
music itself, everyone was on the melody, more or less,
so that the only harmony came in desperate lunges as
someone fell far enough off the pitch to make a momen-
tary, inadvertent third. The tone was heavily adenoidal
with occasional thickenings brought on by a catarrh-
stricken coloratura and a phlegmatic basso. Further tonal
color was added by an abruptly decanting soprano in the
back row whose boyfriend's idea of a Christmas goose
seemed less Dickensian than Benny Hill.

After the one verse of "Silent Night," this Mimeo Chorale went on to "Jingle Bells," an arrangement which
floundered during the "dashing through the snow" apparently owing to there not being enough copies of the
words to go around. . . .

There you are. You are in his unappreciative shoes. He has
won you over, because he tells an interesting story, one with
detail and dialogue. And he tells it with passion.

Notice that this writer's voice is different from his speaking
voice. Had he spoken that night to the Mimeo Chorale he might

have simply told the unharmonious group to bugger off. Here, in a more sedate, more congenial, more understated—if just as passionate—way, he has told you about the various shortcomings of certain modern behavior.

What provided that bridge between simple, angry conversation and lyrical prose? Reflecting on the origins of that piece, Stephen Jones said, "[As a writer] you can go two or three places with anger. Lyricism is one of those places. But you must let your thoughts evolve. It takes time to cycle through emotional phases. In the best cases, lyricism eventually springs from anger, agony, or fear. If on the other hand it springs from lyricism itself, it's too much like Musak."

In the case of the Christmas carol piece, the writer eventually transformed raw feelings into lyrical commentary. He made his point backward, deliciously backward, slowly, carefully, with great reverence for word and thought. He did not stoop to describing in prurient detail the adolescent behavior of the boy in the choir who pinched the girl in a sensitive part of her anatomy. He wrote, instead, the "boyfriend's idea of a Christmas goose seemed less Dickensian than Benny Hill." He used vivid, imaginative descriptions: ". . . one tall goop who held a flashlight which he cast about on the various scripts like a meter man in a strange cellar . . ." But mostly, he was saying that it's more than the thought that counts. It's the detail. It's the work ethic. It's knowing the harmonies, not stumbling upon them. It's caring enough.

These are the things that form the basis of the rich essay—the weaving of the personal observation with reported detail on issues that are significant, if not to the world, then to you. It's up to you to make people care. Had Stephen Jones proposed an essay entitled, "Christmas Carols Aren't Sung as Well as They Used to Be," it would have sounded innocuous, limited, even ridiculous. Instead an event—a metaphorical event—occurred, one with sufficiently amusing detail, that allowed the writer to apply real meaning to the narrative, his point of view, his passionate interpretation. Something happened on the night he was watching television, some spark flickered within him, some notion that what he heard outdoors was in no way harmonious with Christmas eves long ago. "In fact," he says, "the inspiration was thrust upon me. It arrived literally on my doorstep."

ֿוֹh ‎ר‎‎ֿ

The writing voice of Steve Jones is obviously a rich if understated one. It works well for him, but it is a voice that developed over decades. Every writer's voice is different. Compare, for example, Steve's penchant for understatement with the stridency of Roger Eddy's direct approach.

I asked Eddy to write about his unsuccessful campaign in 1986 to unseat Senator Christopher Dodd. Underlying this request was the fact that I knew Eddy as an uncommonly frank politician and a fiction writer of some note. Perhaps he could take us all on the inside of a race. And so he did—so much so, and in so detailed a manner, that it became a three-part series. Much of the series was "action." That is, Eddy brought the reader into behind-the-scenes meetings. And yet the action was selective; it was chosen to enhance Eddy's own point of view, developed and polished after a disillusioning campaign and a brutal beating at the polls. Afterward, he knew his political career was over and that he could now write about it in a way that few politicians have ever been free to do; he could write without worrying whether it would affect a future election. He could tell all. He could tell, for example, how he felt about one of the mainstays of his party. Here is his account of his private meeting with fellow (if maverick) Republican Lowell Weicker, then the senior U.S. senator for Connecticut.

> Later in the office in the Hart Building, after congratulating me and telling me how pleased he was, Lowell Weicker said, "And let me tell you this. I have already informed the press that I plan to act as your statewide chairman. And now I am telling you that I plan to campaign up and down and across the entire state of Connecticut on your behalf. I am going to go all out for you, and I hope you know what that means. Because when Lowell Weicker goes all out for someone, he goes all out.
>
> "And let me tell you something else," he added, wav-

ing aside my attempt to speak. "Let me tell you something else. You are going to win. I know what all these so-called experts have been telling you around Washington, how you don't have a chance and all that baloney. Because I'm telling you," he said, jabbing a finger in my direction, "I'm telling you that you are going to win. And why are you going to win? Because I'm going to campaign for you, that's why. I am going to give you my total and absolute support. And that's why you're going to win."

For the sake of chronology it should be emphasized that this interview took place a few weeks before Lowell Weicker's interview with a reporter from the *New London Day*, who quoted him as saying that anyone who believed that Eddy had a chance to win should have his head examined. It was during that same interview in the *Day* that, for all intents and purposes, Weicker endorsed my opponent for reelection by saying he had an excellent record, almost precisely like his own.

However, when I was with him, he said, "You are going to win. But you've got to run a perfect campaign. And I know about perfect campaigns. I know more about running perfect campaigns than anyone in Connecticut. Hell, I know more about running perfect campaigns than anyone in America."

Here was Eddy telling you what he thinks of his own party's politics simply by describing a *private* scene. Most of the passage is a quote. It is the selection of the quote, and the minimal commentary following it, that reveals Eddy's point of view.

If Eddy was not particularly vulnerable himself, his willingness to reveal such telling detail gave him reader confidence and therefore license to stray temporarily from recounting the narrative into commentary on all matters central or peripheral to the political process. Here, for example, is his view of the press.

While still nurtured by Hollywood and by network television, the image of the "fearless editor"—standing alone and resolute, battling a corrupt establishment, ready and willing to tackle anything and anyone, no matter how powerful and entrenched—is no longer borne out by reality and fact, assuming it ever was.

News . . . has become one of the largest, fastest growing, and most profitable industries in the United States. The last thing a publisher, or a "parent company," wants or needs in an editor is one who upsets readers and advertisers by discussing the truly controversial subjects which divide society.

Indeed, truth can be defined as that which cannot be discussed in the editorial pages of our daily newspapers. Editors know what the truth is, and they certainly must think about it as they drive to and from their homes in the suburbs. But it never appears in their editorials.

I do not say this either in scorn or criticism. Newspaper editors who sidestep the truth, who avoid it, who leave it to those who write fiction, are essential to the preservation of society, which is what peacetime politics is all about. Politics in times of peace is shifting sand, drifting snow, flowing water, metal which melts but never congeals. Politics is noise, millions of human voices all talking at each other and no one listening to anyone except themselves. Peacetime politics has no plot.

Here was a writer who had mastered his material, who clearly knew what he wanted to say. Eddy's writing certainly had plot: he took readers through the entire process. The detail, however, would not have been enough. Eddy's reflections—his conclusions—about this significant episode in his life were what made the piece, were what separated it from the mere accounting of events into an essay, a singular point of view that—because of his experience and his unique viewpoint and his own natural use of the language—could not have been written by anyone else. Politics is a profession of platitudes, the same charge he makes about newspapers. It was a wise use of personal essay

space to assess the two professions frankly, and without regard
to consequence.

Mixing point of view with narrative is a classic fiction technique and one of the characteristics that makes modern nonfiction so compelling. It is so much more meaningful to declare
values and viewpoints than simply to offer plot even if plot, the
moving forward of events toward some compelling climax, is
important. We all knew the punch line of Eddy's memoir: defeat
at the polls. But the journey, the struggle, the illumination along
the way are the real rewards of such a piece. Personal essays, of
course, can be built toward a climax. The most memorable ones
certainly are, and they are reflective of some compelling reason
to write them, and some compelling reason to read them.

გუ ᲠᲔ

When point of view is clearly drawn out of such personal experience, you as a writer have an advantage. You have been living
with these feelings. You merely need a vehicle, a story, in which
to express them, to draw them out, to polish them. But as you
develop your writing, you will see that you often must apply
yourself to questions that have much less obvious answers, to
plumb point-of-view writing when there is ambivalence or even
chaos. It isn't as if you have no point of view—if you didn't you
would not be interested in writing. It is that finding it, standing
behind it, expressing it—these are substantial challenges.

To illustrate, consider the case of a man who had become a
writer with excellent credentials long before I knew him. Bob
Sudyk had been an award-winning columnist in Cleveland, the
coauthor of Hall-of-Fame pitcher Gaylord Perry's autobiography,
and a columnist and sports writer in Hartford.

Baseball, or the periphery of baseball, is what brought us
together. Bob and I had talked about a piece for years that he
had long wanted to write but never had the forum or the time to
develop. He had had a thirty-six-year personal and professional
relationship with George Steinbrenner, who certainly became
one of the most notorious of all sports owners. By then two
unauthorized biographies of Steinbrenner had been written, as

well as thousands of news stories and hundreds of magazine articles. And yet nothing had been written from the perspective of the writer who knew him best—a man who met Steinbrenner in the spring of 1953 when their respective college teams met in Dayton, Ohio, and Bob Sudyk first heard the threats of the bully who was then manager of the University of Dayton nine. This young Steinbrenner said he would pull his team off the field because he wasn't going to play the Ohio State junior varsity. It was all bluff. The game was played. And there began an odd relationship that had staying power.

I suggested that Bob write a sort of reminiscence and profile, a combination. To a certain degree it could be written chronologically. That is, just to lend a structure that certainly suggested itself, he should begin with 1953. We knew that the final version would not begin there, that he would have to offer somewhere high up in the piece a reason for the writing—some conclusions, some clear indication of point of view. But for purposes of narrative and structure, it made sense to begin at the chronological beginning. The real beginning would develop later, and it would be suggested, we hoped, by the content of the narrative, by the interpretation of events.

As this was a nearly four decade relationship, it was not easy for Bob to document. It took him several months to complete the first version, close to ten thousand words. It had compelling elements. It showed George Steinbrenner in ways that neither of the biographies had, because Bob Sudyk had been there during the critical times in Steinbrenner's life: when, against his father's wishes, young George bought the Cleveland Pipers, a team in the fledgling American Basketball League; when he hired the first black head coach in professional sports; when he tried, unsuccessfully, to buy into baseball in Cleveland; when he flew into New York to introduce himself as the new principal owner of the Yankees; when he stood in the locker room after the first World Series victory, looking not behind with satisfaction but ahead with concern and pessimism; when he bought, as he did each morning, fifteen doughnuts and ate three of them on the way to work so that a perfect dozen could be presented to his staff. Bob knew him, too, during the Yankee decline. And,

although the piece was written before Steinbrenner was obliged
to give up control of the Yankees, there had long been signs of
decline in the Yankee organization and in George Steinbrenner's own system of values. The narrative itself was clearly
rich in anecdote. Because Sudyk had been with Steinbrenner on
so many critical occasions—Steinbrenner had even once tried to
get Sudyk fired early in his career with the *Cleveland Press*—it
was not hard for Bob to summon ways to describe each incident.

What was hard was to develop an overall point of view. Certainly the piece was filled with opinion. If, as Bob describes,
there is a scene where Steinbrenner's employees at Yankee
Stadium cower before him, it was easy for Bob to conclude that
Steinbrenner, as a boss, or as The Boss, is a tyrant. That opinion
certainly was verified by making eighteen managerial changes
in eighteen years. But beyond those moments, what would be
the overall viewpoint? What would Bob promise the reader
beyond what had been printed elsewhere? He knew it could not
be just another attempted documentation of an undocumentable
ego; and it would not entice simply because of the personal
relationship alone.

To reach that conclusion took many discussions with Jan
Winburn, *Northeast*'s associate editor, and me, a great deal of
thought on Bob's part, additional reporting, and a number of
rewrites. The answer was partly in Bob, partly in Steinbrenner,
and partly in what Bob had learned was important not only to
luminaries but to every human being: roots. Roots mean values.
And values help writers arrive at point of view. One of Bob's
themes was not George Steinbrenner the tyrant so much as
George Steinbrenner the son of the tyrant. Bob made connec-
tions between father and son that revealed that Henry Steinbrenner had set such high standards for his son that George
could never live up to them, and if he couldn't live up to them,
certainly no manager, and no employee, could. But there was
more that Bob needed to weave between the narrative lines. He
also needed to display a strong theme at the start.

Bob's first top of the piece (remember, he had originally

started the narrative with events that occurred in 1953) was to draw on another scene, this from 1972:

> George is on a Cleveland–New York flight for a press conference to announce his ownership of the New York Yankees. Apprehensive over his acceptance in New York, George plans to enter the Broadway stage humbly, with hat in hand. For now.
>
> "They're going to look at me like I just fell off a wagonload of turnips," he says. "I want to restore this great team to its roots of Gehrig, Ruth and DiMaggio. . . . I want a winner in five years. I want this team to become the greatest in baseball again, a happening."
>
> His timing is right. He is inheriting a faltering fourth-place team from CBS that had drawn less than a million fans for the first time in 29 years. He slips a team picture from his briefcase. "This looks like a poster advocating birth control," he quips. "We got a guy (second baseman Horace Clarke) who wears his batting helmet on defense."
>
> Meanwhile, a nervous stewardess on her first flight fumbles more times than his stone-fingered infield. With the gusto of a first sergeant, George chews her out, takes her name and promises a nasty letter to the airline. She is in tears.
>
> As he deplanes at LaGuardia, an elderly, well-dressed woman passenger jabs him in the back with her umbrella. "That poor girl. Who do you think you are?" she demands.
>
> "We don't need your kind in New York. Why don't you stay in Cleveland where you belong?"

Bob then used this anecdote to launch into what he thought at that time might be his overall point of view:

> George and I, a sports historian of sorts, began our media marriage on a baseball diamond in Lockbourne

Air Force Base 36 springs ago. Our separate but parallel
paths have been weathered by years of angry storms and
pleasurable sunshine. He once tried to have me fired and
sought to put my newspaper out of business. Another
time, he offered me a job and tried to save the same
newspaper when it became financially troubled. And
once, unintentionally, he got me a raise in pay.

He is charming, generous and a delight to be around.
He also can be despotic, impatient, bullying and most
difficult to work for. He is a driven man, forever pushing
himself and those he employs to the edge. After knowing
him for almost four decades, whatever he has been, he
was never boring. What other sports figure has been the
punch line for comic strips "Wizard of Id," "Berry's
World," "Doonesbury" and "Tank McNamara" and
countless television sitcoms? If his team is not happening, he is. . . .

Well, fine. It did what so many pieces do: in a clever capsuli-
zation of what was to come, he could entice the reader simply
with a promise of events. George had once tried to get him
fired? A reader might be intrigued by such a line. Still, it was
merely a preview of coming attractions. It wasn't a real point of
view. That could come only with the answer to this question:
why, after all this time, was Bob writing this story?

It was a question he struggled with. It took another visit to
Yankee Stadium and more thinking time to arrive at an answer.
Bob had to master this enormously rich material in order to
make sense of it. Where is the imminence, the timeliness, the
sense of inevitability of the piece? All of these things—just like
the details of George's life—were clues to the point of view.
When Bob returned from New York that day, he had a new
beginning, a beginning that was the key to his point of view:

Thick leaden clouds skim the treetops flanking Inter-
state 84 as we drive southward toward The City. The
photographer, brimming with sunshine, speaks brightly
about our audience with George M. Steinbrenner III at
his bastille in the Bronx.

"Look," I warn, "I know George. Stopping him for a photograph is like trying to stop a cattle stampede in a thunderstorm."

"I've photographed dozens of CEOs," he says. "They're always in a hurry. You have to take charge. . . . I'll need about 10 minutes to set up," he adds, facing skyward and closing his eyes, no doubt psyching his performance with some positive imagery. "Not to worry, I'll handle him."

I'm thinking, "Whoa boy, I can't wait to see this."

I turn off the Major Deegan Expressway and into Yankee Stadium parking lot 14. We take the elevator to a reception area just outside George's executive office. This is the stadium's communications center. It was soon to become disaster central. Two telephone operators monitor walkie-talkies linking a mini-battalion of Burns Security soldiers in their ankle-length overcoats stationed throughout the stadium.

Anxiety abounds less in anticipation of the exhibition game against the Mets this afternoon than George's first appearance at the stadium this spring. Everyone is busy-busy, moving quickly in and out of the glass doors, dodging each other on appointed routes, giving the place the look of a human anthill.

I'm scheduled to see George at 10 A.M. He is late. It's an ominous sign. . . . George, you see, is never late.

Yankee Stadium will never be mistaken for Camelot. This hectic April Fools' Day morning captures the essence of George Steinbrenner's image. He doesn't just own the New York Yankees, he rules them with fear and a clenched fist. He is viewed as a heartless bully, an impatient taskmaster who pushes himself and others to the brink, a man at the mercy of his emotions, frustrated because he feels he is so misunderstood.

This loose puzzle of a man I have known for almost 40 years once tried to get me fired and then threatened to put my newspaper out of business. He is the same man who came to my wedding, who offered me a job when that same newspaper was in terminal financial condi-

tion, and who has continued to support me during a
career disappointment. The George I know is a real
softy. A caring friend. Sure, he is an unfinished puzzle
with pieces left over that don't fit. But a man who would
kill for jelly bread can't be all bad.

Bob now knew what he wanted to say. He wanted to explore
the difference between the Steinbrenner image and the real
man—or as much as he knew of the real man. He found in
detail hints to the truths that he had been carrying around for
decades. Now Bob had to go beyond telling the reader that he
knew Steinbrenner and that interesting anecdotes would follow;
he had to give some hint of the tension, of the point of view, of
the idea that contradiction would be explored. And he did so in
a clever way, introducing several subplots. There were hints
there that had been revealed in previous versions, such as
George trying to get him fired. But now, aside from the main
exploration of image and reality—the main point of view of the
piece—here was the inherent promise that the writer would deal
with some intriguing milestones and then connect them to his
premise.

Bob used that beginning as a way to set up the next section—
the first section written in the original piece. He bolted back to
1953 to bring people up to date on his relationship with George
as he waited for one last visit with his friend the tyrant. Inherent
in that promised visit was that somewhere along the way, maybe
after Bob recounted the '89 World Series triumph, George would
show up and we would indeed see whether the confident photographer would get his man.

Bob did use the morning's visit—with constant updates on
the approach of The Boss—to weave past and present. Bob
sensed that no matter how strong the anecdotes, it was better to
keep the piece rooted in the here and now. Readers identify that
way. So as he waited for George he described the goings on in
the human anthill, told about how Henry had kicked him out of
his office when he went there to find George in the early 1960s,
how George quietly gives enormous charity donations and
quietly helps friends in times of crisis, and he told of the early

years with the Yankees, and that fateful conversation in the locker room after the World Series win ("You don't seem to be having enough fun," I said. "Win it all once and you've got to keep winning it all," he replied.).

And sure enough, the photography incident finally was described:

In minutes, a little old man is quickly rolling up an all-weather carpet in front of the elevator door out of which George is expected to emerge at any moment. . . . Reports continue:

"He's going into the Stadium Club now."

"He's not going to like that either."

I remark to one of the operators, "I don't work for George, and I feel tension."

He's been through this before. He smiles and replies, "The temperature's rising."

For the first time the confident photographer has a worried look on his face.

Two young men with vacuum sweepers roar into the reception room at full throttle and then into George's office. It's swept every 15 minutes when he is in the ball park.

Suddenly, the elevator door jerks open and George comes out smoking from his full house inspection. He is behind schedule and says he'll meet me after the game. I ask for a couple of minutes for the photographers.

"OK, but make it snappy," he replies.

The photographer enters his spacious office where a meeting is about to begin. He is fumbling nervously with his equipment, trying to assemble his camera faster than he knows how. He wants a Polaroid shot to check the lighting.

"C'mon, are you guys ready?" presses George. "Do it now or forget it."

By now, the photographer is completely unglued. He is dropping lenses and other accessories onto the floor. "Ready," he says haltingly, as if he is not so sure.

Predictably, George takes over the filming.

"Take three here," he orders. Click-click-click. "Take a couple here next to Babe Ruth's picture." Click-click. "Take a few over here." Click-click-click.

"That's it," says George. "You got enough. I've got work to do."

We leave and the photographer, looking like he has just fallen down a flight of stairs, says "I've never been through anything like this in my life. I'm not sure I set the camera right. I don't think I got a thing. This has never happened to me before."

His face is ashen. Steinbrenner intimidation has swallowed up another victim. The overwhelmed photographer takes a train back to Hartford. I sit down in the press box to watch the Mets and Yankees in their final tuneup for the '89 regular season. Gate receipts will go to a number of New York charities.

A clever juxtaposition at the end—tyranny and charity. Moreover, Bob continued to express his clear reason for the piece, his clear point of view: firsthand knowledge of that tyranny and charity. This, then, is the promise to the reader, the point of view, the argument, the persuasion. The reason for the piece.

Now, looking back on the piece and on what has happened to Steinbrenner since that time, the end of the piece seems ironic, and fitting.

His shoes now shined, he inspects himself before a mirror. He runs a comb through his hair, signaling that another meeting is coming to a close.

"I'll never sell the team," he says. "It's a tremendous challenge. It's fun and keeps me young. My good friend, Harry Mangurian, regrets the day he sold the Boston Celtics. They are a tradition in basketball like the Yankees in baseball. There would be a terrible void in my life without the Yankees. I want the kids to take over someday. But I'm a long way from stepping out to pasture myself. . . . So are you, pal. . . ."

♃ 5 ♌

Once Upon a Time. Really.

The Narrative Approach to Nonfiction

When Roger Eddy, a candidate for the U.S. Senate who came up empty and fuming, wrote that newspapers "leave the truth for fiction writers," he was contending that, while much of modern reporting may get a reasonable percentage of the facts straight, the underlying meaning of those facts is still elusive. Newspapers contain no shortage of "he said" and "she said" and "expert says"; nor, in pieces that pretend to relate the human struggle, do they lack for terms meant to evoke emotional reactions, such as "nightmare" or "struggle" or the ever-popular "ordeal." This is journalistic shorthand, and shorthand is never as effective as the real thing—fully drawn stories that offer insight, depth, narrative, and rich characterization.

Newspapers like to say they present a "balanced" view. What they really do is present an agreeable set of alternatives. That is, if dark is reported, equal space must be given to light. It is as if there were no such thing as news, only the appearance of news and of opposite viewpoints—in the interest of "fairness."

If, for example, a newspaper had been produced by Adam and Eve and they followed modern journalistic practices, issue number one of the *Garden of Eden Daily Bugle* might have run the following banner headline: "Reaction Is Mixed to the News of the Earth's Creation." The story might read, "A poll taken of the earth's two residents indicates that 50 percent of the population thinks the world is a very fine idea and 50 percent would rather reserve judgment, seeing as how in the first few days of his existence he already reports the loss of a rib."

Therefore, the *Garden of Eden Daily Bugle* would have proved by "objective" reporting that the earth's creation was a questionable undertaking. Meaningful writing about such matters happens to appear in the form of a narrative that begins, "In the beginning . . ." The Bible is an early example of narrative— a narrative that certainly weaves point of view among significant events.

This is not to suggest that you fill your pieces with "begat" and "cubit" and "smote," but if religion traces its beginnings to the creation of the earth, writing traces its beginnings to the creation of the narrative—the fictional equivalent to "In the beginning," which is also a phrase from your childhood: "Once upon a time . . ."

Until relatively recently, "Once upon a time" writing was the province only of fiction writers. These fortunate souls have traditionally been encumbered only by the limits of their imaginations, and have been free to explore both circumstance and emotion that lead to the sort of headlines that intrigue and baffle us. They are free, too, to construct a narrative that engages the reader.

Fiction structure did not suite newspapers, whose primary "style" was to tell stories backward: the so-called inverted pyramid approach. Information was the point—and it should go right at the top of the pieces. Although in the lingo of the newsroom these pieces are called "stories," they are anything but. A story needs a beginning, middle, and end. It must put the reader into the action, into the emotion.

Journalism in Sunday magazines and other serious journals has come to resemble fiction in that writers combine eye for detail, ear for revealing dialogue, excellent reporting, and passion for the human condition with classic story-telling techniques. The result is a hard edge that nevertheless contains within it introspection and interpretation.

For an editor, teaching people to write "once upon a time" pieces that are rooted in real life is a rewarding process, and it provides growth and challenge for writers. After she was awarded her Pulitzer Prize in 1986, police reporter Edna Buchanan wrote to me, "I still consider the Amy Billig piece I did for you [a nonfiction narrative about a missing teenager] among the best work I have done." It is also safe to say that if readers are touched by personal essays, they are also richly rewarded by the powerful nonfiction narrative, because it combines the most appealing aspects of story telling—getting to know the primary characters, and caring about those characters—with a story that contains all the classic fiction guideposts: exposition, conflict, and climax among them. In addition, it offers the sort of reporting on timely issues that is not necessarily pervasive in modern fiction.

Jim Ricci, who went on to develop the Writing Enrichment program at the *Detroit Free Press*, recalls his first nonfiction narrative for *Beacon*, in which he provided the chronology of a natural childbirth, which in 1972 was an unusual phenomenon. Rather than do a "survey" piece, the popular genre of the time, he decided instead to focus on one couple, Leonard and Martha DeJulius, and to follow them from childbirth classes through the birth itself. His idea was that, by getting to know the DeJuliuses, the reader would have a stake in their lives and in the birth of their child. Jim could both tell the story of the birth and weave in, at critical points along the way, reporting on the subject of natural childbirth, so that the story of the DeJuliuses had a context, a perspective.

The piece began with labor pains seven minutes apart, immediately announcing to readers impending birth. Then Jim digressed, introducing Leonard G. DeJulius:

> [He is] 48, a small, dark, muscular man with distinct Mediterranean features and a quiet voice. He is a dentist specializing in the treatment of children and, as such, understands pain.
>
> When his wife, Martha, 21, learned she was pregnant, she resolved to have the baby without medication or anesthesia; to give birth naturally. It was up to her, and Lenny quickly agreed. "The closer you can get to nature, the better off you are."

After describing the preliminaries at the hospital, Jim introduced the personal histories of Leonard and Martha. Jim wrote
what he saw:

> The doctor sat on a low stool leaning back against a
> wall, his arms folded and his legs extended and crossed
> in front of him. Nurses Kaiser, Cathleen Sullivan and
> Adeline Griffith quietly busied themselves with minor
> preparations at various tables and stands on the room's
> periphery. It was not quite time yet.
>   Center stage was Martha's. She lay atop the high table,
> her limbs quivering and her facial muscles flexing and
> unflexing with the ebb and flow of the pain. Lenny
> stood behind her head. His hands cupped Martha's face.
> Quiet reigned save for Martha's occasional sobs as the
> child inside her inched painfully along its critical jour-
> ney.
>   The pain and the sobbing made it hard for her to
> control her breathing. Unable to continue the subdued
> accelerated-decelerated breathing, she switched to blow-
> ing hard through pursed lips to fight the enormous urge
> to push, to bear down on her abdominal muscles, force
> the baby out before it was ready.

Reporting more of the painful and anxiety-ridden preliminaries, the details of Leonard's "staccato of encouragement,"
and Martha's one last refusal of painkillers, Jim prepared the
readers for the moment of birth:

> Amid the quiet tinkering and business talk among the
> medical people at the foot of the table, a sharp, irritated
> wail shot upward.
>   Laura Ann DeJulius, seven pounds, three ounces, 20
> inches long, 5:43 A.M.—freed from the confines of her
> old world—sucked in her first lungful of air and let fly
> one prolonged, glorious complaint at her new world. The
> sun was out and, as it exited, it sent one last heat wave
> through Martha.

Jim now reflects, "It was the first chronology I ever undertook, the first time I followed something from beginning to end. It required arranging complete access, which is not easy to do, and then, in effect, baby-sitting the emerging events, and letting them happen before my eyes. This technique is what I came to call creative reporting. Don't just ask people what they think. Arrange to see things. Notice the color of the walls and the way the place smells. Notice the bracelet on the husband's arm as he holds the wife's hand in the operating room. And there is nothing so compelling in a story as live dialogue between actual people. Whenever you're not there, you're losing something. You should inscribe the words 'Go there' on your typewriter."

ᴕᴕ ᴕᴕ

Perhaps the most telling illustration of the "Go there" philosophy was a certain train trip to Washington, D.C., in the summer of 1979, embarked upon by eighty-three-year-old Edward Zepp and writer Madeleine Blais.

Edward Zepp had become a regular in south Florida newsrooms, arguing on his own behalf, largely to unsympathetic ears. The reporters had heard it all before: how Mr. Zepp, at least in his own eyes, had been denied justice six decades earlier and ever since by the Pentagon. As a young soldier in World War I, he had been sent to France and had refused to fight, claiming that he was a conscientious objector. A court-martial was held and Zepp was sentenced to confinement at Leavenworth and a dishonorable discharge from the army. Although the remainder of his life seemed to have turned out quite honorably—he became head of a prominent Cleveland charity—he was never able to persuade the Pentagon of his devout belief in nonviolence. The best it would do was upgrade the discharge from dishonorable to general in 1951, a gesture that did not satisfy Zepp. When the old man's wife was on her deathbed, he promised her that he would clear his name, and that he would get his honorable discharge. In a few weeks he would plead his case in person at the Pentagon; it would be his last chance.

Such was the pertinent background. Now came the decision

as to how to report and tell the story. To Madeleine Blais and to me, the only sensible way was to be on the train with Zepp as he went to make his last appeal in Washington. It was a natural. Here was what appeared to be a gentle, if stubborn, old man, fighting to clear his name against difficult odds. Whatever the outcome, it would be a good story, one that could explore significant subjects such as aging, conscientious objection, bureaucracy, and personal commitment told in the framework of a compelling narrative.

Maddy recalls: "The thing about that story that worked so well was that it was, in fact, a journey. The material had its own shape. It was really a series of journeys. There was the present-day trip on the train, a finite, contemporary time—and there was a journey backward, from 1979 to 1917. It was also a spiritual journey, the mental and psychological process of what this man had been going through. The power of the piece derived from the feeling of motion that all those journeys created."

In preparing to write the story, Maddy read Erich Maria Remarque's novel of World War I, *All Quiet on the Western Front.* From it she not only acquired a more spiritual sense of the time, but took particular note of its narrative sweep. She was convinced that good journalism and literature could have much in common. "I formulated that idea that journalism didn't have to be a compendium of quotes coming at you." It can be, in short, a good story.

It was in the details of Maddy's reporting—her eyes—that Edward Zepp's campaign came alive and meaningful. Here is how she began, describing Zepp on the train to Washington:

> All his life Edward Zepp has wanted nothing so much as to go to the next world with a clear conscience. So on September 11 the old man, carrying a borrowed briefcase filled with papers, boarded an Amtrak train in Deerfield Beach and headed north on the Silver Meteor to our nation's capital. As the porter showed him to his roomette, Ed Zepp kept saying, "I'm eighty-three years old. Eighty-three."
>
> At 9 A.M. the next day, Zepp was to appear at the

Pentagon for a hearing before the Board for Correction of Military Records. This was, he said, "the supreme effort, the final fight" in the private battle of Private Zepp, Company D, 323rd Machine Gun Battalion, veteran of World War I, discharged on November 9, 1919—with dishonor.

Something happens to people after a certain age, and the distinctions of youth disappear. The wrinkles conquer, like an army. In his old age, Zepp is bald. He wears fragile glasses. His shoulders are rounded. His pace is stooped and slow. It is hard, in a way, to remove sixty years, and picture him tall, lanky, a rebel.

The old man, wearing a carefully chosen business suit which he hoped would be appropriately subdued for the Pentagon, sat in a chair of his roomette as the train pulled out of Deerfield Beach. With a certain palsied eagerness he foraged his briefcase. Before the train reached full speed, he arranged on his lap the relics from his days at war. There were the dog tags and draft card, even his Department of War Risk life insurance policy. There was a letter to his mother written in 1919 in France, explaining why he was in the stockade. His fingers, curled with arthritis and in pain, attacked several documents. He unfurled the pages of a copy of the original court-martial proceedings that found him in violation of the 64th Article of War: failure to obey the command of a superior officer. There was also a copy of the rule book for Leavenworth, where Zepp had been sentenced to ten years at hard labor.

The reader was enticed immediately into the story in a way that no shorthand would have done. Words such as "nightmare" or "ordeal" cannot compare with putting the reader in the place of the writer, sitting right next to the old man, seeing precisely what she was seeing. Maddy let the story unfold before her, and she also wove into the narrative her observations about old age—for example, "the distinctions of youth disappear." This is the technique of Remarque, of Mark Twain, of William Make-

peace Thackeray, and of Jane Austen. For nonfiction writers, it
requires the combination of imaginative scene setting and reporting—being there, or reconstructing as if you were there.

৩৮ ৫৫

The narrative then went on to backtrack into Zepp's life, juxtaposing a vulnerable old man and a rebellious youth. In this
journey, Maddy pointed out Zepp's tendency to tell the story
over and over again to everyone he met. This allowed Maddy to
spread the history out, not concentrate it in one place and
interrupt the modern narrative. That is, the train trip, which was
the structure of the piece, was never left for long. The terrors of
the war and Zepp's revelations and descriptions, including the
sergeant putting a gun to his head ordering him to fight, the
denial of facing his accuser at trial, and the horrible conditions
of prison, became chapters between Daytona Beach, St. Augus-
tine, Savannah, and Richmond.

This technique also set up a natural climax: Zepp facing a
formidable task a thousand miles to the north. He would testify
before a triumvirate at the Pentagon, and the burden of proof
would be on him.

> Next the old man took his turn. The panel urged him to
> remain seated during his testimony. The old man mar-
> shalled the highlights of his military experience:
> Shanghaied, nice soft easy job, tactful and courteous
> officer, hard-boiled sergeant, gun at my head, face my
> accusers, unfit for human habitation, unsolicited recom-
> mendation. The words tumbled out, a litany. . . .
>
> Every now and then Zepp's composure cracked, stall-
> ing the proceedings. "I'm sure it's hard to recall," said [a
> panel member].
>
> "It's not that," said the defendant. "I'm just living it.
> This was indelibly impressed, it is vivid on my mind, like
> something that happened yesterday."
>
> That afternoon was more of the same: Lt. Herbert was
> not making me a sincere offer, German sympathizer,
> disgrace your sisters, sincere religious objections. . . .

[Zepp says:] "The one thing that bothers me is my conscience, my allegiance to the Almighty. I have to see this thing through. . . . I don't think that a person who follows the dictates of his conscience and is a true Christian should be stigmatized as a dishonorable person. And I think he shouldn't even get a second-rate discharge.

"And the reason I'm here at my advanced age—eighty-three, arthritis and all that—my inner self, my conscience says, 'Now here. You go to the board and make one last effort,'" Zepp paused. He hunched forward and made ready to sling one final arrow: "In view of the fact . . . there's not much difference, then why not make it honorable? There isn't much difference. Let's make it honorable and we'll all be happy."

The panel closed the proceedings. A decision was promised sometime within the next month.

The last part of the piece—and it was carefully reserved for the end—was the Pentagon's decision. When the word finally came, it was in the form of a Pentagon statement, a copy of which was sent to Zepp's condo. It acknowledged that he had indeed been a conscientious objector in 1919 and accordingly awarded him, after six decades, his honorable discharge.

You would think the story would be over. But Maddy duly recorded the ironic kicker—the surprise that all good stories, narrative or not, offer readers. That surprise is inevitable if a writer keeps eyes and ears open, because no fiction can come close to the ironies of real life. Here is the end of the story of the man who all his life had argued that he opposed violence:

[Mr. Zepp] discovered the decision was not unanimous. One member . . . had voted against him. "I'm so mad I could kick the hell out of him. . . . I'd like to go up there and bust his head wide open."

Here was a dramatic, shocking ending, but it only shows the possibilities of surprise and illumination when the writer is present. Surprise is what sticks with a reader, and a writer does well to record his or her own surprises. They will certainly translate to the reader.

Now here is the surprise kicker to the story of the *writing* of Edward Zepp's journey.

৸ ৻৻

Before Maddy began writing for me, and before I hired her as a staff writer for *Tropic*, she had been a reporter for the *Trenton Times*. Her goal at the time was to land a job at the *Washington Post*. She sent off a résumé and, as custom dictates, a selection of clippings illustrating her work. The *Post* considered the package, and passed the work among senior editors for their comments. Each wrote a short memo with his or her assessment. Unfortunately—or fortunately for me, because Maddy would never have arrived at my office doorstep—one of the notes was not retrieved before the package and the polite rejection were put in the mail.

It was a very negative evaluation of Maddy's work and potential. So you can imagine the feeling that she must have had on receiving it. And you can also imagine the feeling she had when, in the spring of 1980, Madeleine Blais, who, according to someone at the *Washington Post*, "has no perceptible talent," received the Pulitzer Prize for Feature Writing for her story of Edward Zepp and for four other excellent magazine pieces.

৸ ৻৻

Access to the subject—so critical to Maddy and other writers of nonfiction narrative—is the primary source of that critical sense of surprise, that illumination that is a direct result of the writer's keen sense of observation.

You have read, no doubt, many stories about the homeless. But consider this paragraph from a narrative by Bob Sudyk on the life of Albert and Kandy Leduc, river nomads, people who live along the shore and who venture into the city for their daily needs:

First stop is G. Fox (a department store), where Kandy

sprays herself with sample perfumes, and Albert combs his hair in the mirror with free hair tonic. "There's a hotel bar that has cocktail hour buffet TGIF nights," he says. "We can turn a $2.50 bottle of beer into an evening meal."

Obviously, the sort of access that Bob Sudyk and Jim Ricci were counseling and the sort that gave Maddy Blais the opportunity to report such a compelling story about Edward Zepp is not always available. Sometimes the story has to be investigated and reconstructed without the benefit of Being There. Such technique requires the reconstructive eye—and all varieties of reporting, digging, reading, seeing, and sensing.

Underlying the nonfiction narrative, certainly, is the feeling that no headline can tell an entirely true story, and so much information bombards readers today that even the most extraordinary facts bounce off. They are unaffecting. The intent of the nonfiction narrative is to wait until the news occurs, then go behind the headlines to reconstruct events in a meaningful way. One objection some writers have to subjects is that "they have already been covered." But I never think that way until I cover it in the magazine. It may be a conceit, but it is surely one that has led to meaningful work far more often than not.

The majority of the nonfiction narratives that have appeared over the years were suggested by the news. On nearly every day's front page is some inspiration for a piece with greater depth—for the *real* story. Even if the subject is a fairly dense one, there is great opportunity to explore, to explain, to apply human emotion to every phenomenon of significance.

Identifying the subject, however, is the easy part. Finding the proper focus is a more difficult matter. Sometimes as much time is taken deciding upon whom the piece will center as on the actual reporting and writing.

It is true that some focuses suggest themselves. Early in a string of very effective nonfiction narratives for *Northeast*, Robin Finn explored the topic of drunk driving by centering on a single accident. The piece was enormously powerful in its detail and emotion. And yet, to some degree, any accident might have been chosen. The subject of drunk driving is an emotionally loaded one, and almost any story, provided that story can be reconstructed in detail, can provide the framework for a serious examination of the subject.

But when Robin turned to the subject of the clogged civil courts and the fact that most cases took more than five years to come to trial, we had a problem. It was a subject crying out to be examined in that it affected thousands of people and signaled a breakdown in the judicial system. And yet, for all of its significance, it could be deadly dull if not done in the right way, if not focused on the right case.

It is a common practice in the nonfiction narrative to weave the human story with the general framework of the subject—the reason for the story. A writer must report both the specifics of the person's life and the details of the subject matter itself. That juxtaposition, that weaving, is the essence of the narrative. Using only one without the other can be fatal to the piece, which will be either entirely lacking perspective, and therefore significance, or too dry.

In the story of the civil courts, the alternating part of the reporting—the number of cases, the interviews with judges and lawyers and plaintiffs and defendants and observers of the legal system—did not suggest any particular challenge in reporting. But what would be the human part of the story? That's where the real digging came in. Dozens of cases had to be examined until the proper one could be found, the one that lent inherent drama to the subject of delay.

After weeks of interviewing lawyers and studying court documents, Robin uncovered the ideal case to write about. Mary Gay had brought a malpractice suit against a doctor following the birth of her son. It was her contention that brain damage had been caused by improper birthing procedures. The damage was of the type that caused eventual deterioration of mental processes so that, while the child at age three had retained much of his mental capacity, his condition would soon deteriorate and would be irreversible. Treatment and corrective action, however, were possible if undertaken quickly. Without a ruling or a settlement, however—and the insurance company appeared unwilling to settle—Mary Gay could not afford the treatment, leaving her son's fate to the sad state of judicial affairs. The case of the mother and child had inherent drama, and it allowed Robin to weave in the causes and consequences of the civil court logjam. By choosing the right focus, she brought a dense and perhaps uncompelling subject to life.

That Mary Gay's situation had inherent drama was certainly helpful to Robin in this case, but it would be wrong to generalize that a writer should always settle on a story with extraordinary circumstances. That case walked the line of being too unusual; if so, it could be easily dismissed by readers as not pertinent to the main problem. It is important for the writer to find a circumstance that is both interesting and metaphorical—one that can stand for many other stories.

After the subject is settled on comes the reporting. This part is most critical; it is really the underpinning of the nonfiction narrative. If a writer has indeed chosen to address a subject with this form, there can be no holes in the reporting. Every side of the story must be uncovered so that, in the telling, the writer can be authoritative.

If a news story is reported largely in the voice of the reporter's sources—filled with "police said" and "officials say" and "sources told the newspaper"—the nonfiction narrative has, as its primary source, the writer. The writer is the one expert on all sides of the story. That is not to say that the writer never uses attribution. In his superb nonfiction narrative *Looking for a Ship*, John McPhee employs the phrase "according to" in one instance. But only once. And of course he quotes many people in the course of the story. But he makes a distinction between quotable material—which contributes to the color and texture of the story—and verifiable facts. In the course of his reporting, many sources offered him "facts" about the nature of modern shipping, or about other people, but these representations did not find their way into the book until the writer had checked their veracity. He then had the perspective of both keen observer and verifier of information, an authority that allows for direct and fluent story telling.

In the normal course of such story telling, you as the writer do not need permission to reveal a narrative. Your exhaustive research and your investment in making sense of the chronology of events gives you that license. You as the writer and reporter become the authority. You become the one person with the depth of knowledge on the subject at hand, as well as the instincts and tools, to make sense of the events. As narrator you must offer the reader the overview, the specifics, the real thinking in the piece.

This requires flawless reporting. It requires that you know much more about the person or the events that you are writing about than will ever see print. Maddy Blais, who is now a professor of journalism at the University of Massachusetts, says, "For a good magazine piece, you throw out 90 percent of what you know. For a newspaper feature, you use 110 percent of what you know. That's the difference."

৯৸ ৶৻

One of the key elements in the reporting process is gaining interviews with the principals in the case. It is safe to say that the more delicate the subject, the more compelling the issue, the more public interest there is in a story, the harder it is to find universal acceptance of your appeal for interviews. Getting people to open up is difficult, time-consuming, and sometimes a discouraging business. But it almost always can be done. Over the years, writers on the magazines I have edited have shown a certain tenacity at this critical skill, and with very rare exceptions have been successful at getting people to talk.

This is not to say they always relish the prospect. When Patricia Weiss undertook a narrative about a most unusual circumstance—the seven-year hiding out amid respectable suburbanites of a man considered by the FBI to be a mob underboss—she knew that for the piece to succeed she had to talk to those suburbanites, none of whom had spoken to the press and only a few of whom were even identifiable. And to make it a first-rate piece she had to speak to Alfonse Persico, the reputed underboss, himself. Persico, however, had *never* talked to the press, a practice in keeping with the normal behavior of organized crime figures. He had not even spoken publicly when he was convicted of taking the life of another man in Manhattan years before.

This was the ultimate test of Pat's theory that deep down everyone wants to talk, everyone wants to tell his or her story. How did she do it? Mostly by showing up.

She decided that the key was Persico's girlfriend, the person who had known him best throughout his years in Hartford. Pat visited her in person, unannounced. At first the girlfriend was angry—tired of being badgered by the press and suspicious of Pat. She asked why she should tell Pat anything. "I gave her a perfectly honest and ultimately persuasive reply," Pat recalls. "I was going to have to write the story with or without her cooperation; the only way she could influence what I said in the piece was to tell me her side of it. She changed her mind several times, but eventually spoke quite candidly."

Pat's success at getting sources to talk seemed to hinge on doing it in person. "I discovered early on that people found it easy to hang up on me if I telephoned. They were more receptive when confronted face-to-face, although this was a time-consuming process. It required that I appear on people's doorsteps in the early evening, around dinnertime, when they were most likely to be home."

Talking in person had other benefits, led down other avenues. "When I was talking to Persico's girlfriend, I got a major break when she mentioned some letters from West Hartford residents had been written on Persico's behalf to the federal judge in Brooklyn who was slated to sentence Persico. The judge's law clerk agreed to let us copy the letters, and I had it done quickly before she could change her mind."

Pat spent the next few weeks tracking down the letter writers and visiting everywhere Persico had lived, every store or bar he might have frequented. "The new residents of his former apartments and houses all let me in reluctantly and ended up giving me the grand tour as though I'd been dispatched by *Metropolitan Home*."

She staked out one house in Newington, Connecticut, for two afternoons. The owners, Persico's best friends, had hung up on other reporters. "I ended up sitting in their kitchen as the wife yapped for an hour while cooking dinner. Then her husband came home and took up the thread of the story. Another couple in Bristol were not quite as accommodating. 'Do you make a habit of barging in on people while they're eating dinner?' the wife demanded. The honest answer would be, 'Habit? It's part of my nightly routine.'

"I didn't get too far with that couple, but I learned that what is true in most other cases is also true of people involved in dramatic news events: despite their better judgment, they're dying to talk. A reporter just has to get them going, maybe with a few unexpected, sympathetic, or very specific questions, then try to keep them going until they're completely played out."

Pat never took out a tape recorder—it was sure to scare a reluctant subject—and the night Persico's girlfriend opened up, "I didn't even take notes until I could see she had begun to relax."

Sometimes wild goose chases turned into strikes of gold. "I think what makes a magazine piece, or any serious piece, is all the extra legwork involved. I explored every lead I got in order to fill in the rich details that suggest you've been there and know what you're talking about. The owners of Persico's favorite Chinese restaurant couldn't remember his favorite dish, but the owners of the Silo in Farmington recalled, 'He liked his pasta,' especially with anchovies and garlic. The superintendent at his last apartment, who cleaned up after his arrest, described everything that had been in the refrigerator. Sometimes details like that never get into the story, but it helps when you're sitting down to write about someone to know what brand of butter he used (Land O'Lakes)."

There was, of course, no chance the fugitive would speak to Pat directly. But then no chance turned into some chance through Pat's persistence—it became clear to him that everyone was spilling the beans, and perhaps unsavory beans at that. It might be in his best interest to talk. Pat and Al Persico had their first telephone interview. Eventually he agreed to see her in person. He opened up to her so much and so often that his life story became a three-part series, one that showed the detailed life of a mobster on the run.

Pat, who seems to be a shy person, has become an expert on the hostile witness. Even though she prefers seeing hostile interviewees in person, she can even get them to talk on the phone. Often she will get someone on the line who refuses to talk to her but will take an hour saying so. Pat will listen sympathetically and ignore the talker's insistence that she doesn't want to talk. After all, she *is* talking.

Such technique is required because every principal in a narrative must be heard from in one way or another. If the writer is "the expert" on the subject, the writer must offer testimony from all sides. Often beginning writers conclude that conflicting reports make for narrative trouble. Nothing seems to fit. But conflict contributes to the richness of the story. And it makes the story more believable, more reflective of real life.

In the nonfiction narrative there is no substitute for detail. And detail is a product of interviews and observation.

When Pat undertook to write another crime story (she has a reputation for suggesting and writing such pieces) about the biggest news in Hartford in 1989—that a prominent developer had apparently murdered his wife and two grown children, then turned the gun on himself—she immediately found roadblocks in the exclusive neighborhood of Woodside Circle.

No one would talk, at least at first. By investigating the periphery during this time—that is, subjects who were not family members but who might have something to say, such as neighbors and estate liquidators—word soon got around, as it always does, that a persistent reporter is going to get a story. Eventually this demonstration convinces subjects to talk because they fear their point of view will not be represented in the piece.

Pat's reconstruction of the life and death of John Cotter and his family was not, in a sense, a classic narrative. Because the principals in the story were dead, and no one could really know for certain the details of what had happened during the four days between the first death and the final one, the narrative took a more metaphorical approach in that it was content with learning as much as possible about the four family members as the story line headed in the general direction, if not the specif-

ics, of the deaths. What emerged from the detail that was uncovered was a point of view—a picture of a family that seemed
much more interested in appearances than in the values that
might have prevented the tragedy:

> Most striking was Anne Cotter's passion for cookbooks.
> She owned 1,200 to 1,500. No less lavish was her table-
> ware collection. She always had a theme when she threw
> a party, and would often buy plates, serving dishes, and
> table linens to match. As a result, she didn't own the
> usual eight settings of china. She owned settings for 12
> to 20 instead, in at least a dozen patterns. Drawers were
> filled with $130 placemats that had not been used. She
> had enough cooking gadgets to fill an issue of the Wil-
> liams-Sonoma catalog.
>
> A consistently stylish if traditional dresser, Anne also
> had closets, racks, and entire rooms bulging with bou-
> tique-style garb. One closet was reserved for linen
> clothes in shades of white and beige. A large armoire
> was stacked with nothing but sweaters. Compulsive
> about color coordination, she also stockpiled scarves,
> pocketbooks, and other accessories. Many outfits were
> hung with plastic bags bearing the matching scarf, jew-
> elry, pantyhose, and even shade of lipstick. . . .

This was no mere voyeurism, as it might have seemed. It fit a
sad puzzle of a family that no longer had the resources to keep
up appearances, an issue that was critical in the end.

 _sh_   _ne_

The structure of the nonfiction narrative is worth an examination. There is no real formula to it, no unbendable rule, unless
you consider this question: what method may be used both to
impart significant information and to keep people reading?
Maddy Blais says that very often there is nothing mystical about
it. Very often it can be a very simple structure. "Chronology,"
she points out, "is structure."

If we begin with the premise that a good story starts in the
beginning, has a middle, and then ends, we begin with a good

premise. However, a nonfiction narrative differs from fiction in that if it based on the news—if it has an imminence to it—pure beginnings, middles, and ends sometimes must be interrupted. These intruders are guideposts, or directions for the reader. This is not always the case, of course. Nothing is *always* the case in writing. If you are writing for *The New Yorker* about why a building's 220 years of history has significance today, it is not necessary to give any indications, other than very subtle ones, early in the piece about such impact. Such a piece may show its purest chronological narrative form: beginning in the eighteenth century and taking the reader to modern times.

You must always know your audience, and, in this case, the audience is a built-in one: to some degree, it will stick with a piece simply because it knows that, in its sophisticated reading experience, it has found that *The New Yorker* seldom disappoints. There is bound to be a payoff. But when writing for a general audience, the writer must convince the reader to invest time, and it can be a much trickier matter. The reader must be told the significance of the piece, and yet the narrative must retain its power, its hold on the reader.

It is fair to say that whether the piece begins in the present or in the past, with the specific story or with an overview, it is certain that the reason for the piece has to come through clearly. Sometimes that reason can be very cleverly displayed in the expository portion of the piece. The beginning of the piece is of course critical in that it must immediately engage readers. So it is generally a good idea to make the beginning as human as possible. But where does the point belong? Where is what journalists call the "nut graph"—the essence of the piece boiled down to one crucial paragraph? In the most effective writing, such a nut graph is metaphorical. The point is filtered, it is inherent in the exposition, it is related by a confident, authoritative writer—by a writer who knows clearly where to take the reader.

Sometimes the nut graph, or nut graphs, can be so entertaining and engaging that they can actually be up front. Consider this example by David Sherwood, in a *Northeast* piece entitled "The Mysterious Mr. Smith":

When David Bushnell Smith died of heart failure on
November 12, 1985, in the single room he rented in
Hartford, the undertaker couldn't learn much about him.
Part of Smith's death certificate reads: City and State of
Birth, Unavailable; Married, Unavailable; Last Spouse,
Unavailable; Usual Occupation, Unavailable; Business,
Unavailable; Father, Unavailable; Mother, Unavailable.

It may as well have read Unremarkable, for nothing
immediately distinguished David Bushnell Smith from
thousands who die alone and poor and without personal
accomplishment.

It could have read Uninteresting, too, or Who Cares?
There seemed no reason to look for the facts of David's
life. But then keys were found in his room. Keys to two
storage bins in a Hartford warehouse. And the bins were
loaded.

A lawyer was made administrator of David's estate by
the probate court. He asked Alice Kugelman, a West
Hartford appraiser, to put a price tag on David's possessions—a three-week task which was "equal to the biggest transaction I've had in my professional life," she
says.

And then there were auctions. Alice had to ask herself
how this man, who claimed net worth of $600 in 1982
and $150 in 1984, could possess, for instance, a falling-
off-the-frame oil canvas of a boy on a riverbank that sold
at auction for $6,500. And where would he get an eigh-
teenth-century book of exotic bird engravings by Ger-
man artist Johann Michael Seligman . . . that fetched
$7,500? . . .

What about the porcelain and ivory, the carved wood,
Wedgwood, rare jewelry, cut glass, bronze and brass
treasures, not to mention lithographs, maps, phonograph
records, pencil sketches, political cartoons?

It all went at auction for $100,012.50. But where'd it
come from? Why was it in storage? And what about the
rumor that David may have been an FBI agent? Or the
other one: that he had written something saying if cer-

tain possessions of his were sold, there could be trouble? And how come he was living at St. Elizabeth House, a shelter for the homeless?

Alice writes for *Northeast.* Writes about antiques, not mysteries. When *Northeast* editors heard of David, they knew there was a mystery here worth exploring, if someone had time to do it.

I had the time.

Well, there is your exposition, your nut graph, and a wonderful enticement to continue. Detail, you see, is much more compelling than promises such as "ordeal" or "odyssey" or "adventure." Such an enticement implies that the writer will indeed deliver. So it may go without saying, except as this is a writing book I had better say it, that promises—or great beginnings—are not enough. Or to put it in a more positive way, David was able to write such a compelling beginning with such authority because he knew he had the goods on David Bushnell Smith. And the reader certainly sensed from reading those few paragraphs that the writer not only had the time—but got results.

ॐ ॐ

You must remember as a writer that your reputation and the reputation of the publication ride on the accuracy of your findings and on the careful conclusions that you make.

Perhaps no writer's body of work better demonstrates those values—and is more illuminating in the matter of critical story telling—than that of Joel Lang.

Joel is a recipient of the highly competitive Master Reporter Award, given to only one New England writer each year for a career's worth of work, largely on the basis of his serious, interpretive pieces. If there is one writer who demonstrates the worth of going behind the headlines, of ferreting out the real motivations that set up the chain of events that eventually end up as shocking headlines, Joel is that practitioner.

In the case of the narrative that Joel wrote about the abortion issue in Connecticut, he stated clearly at the top the reason for the piece because the point was so compelling: How, in a largely Catholic state, did the legislature pass such a liberal abortion law?

There are many examples of narratives that Joel has written where the reason for the piece is not clearly stated in so many words at the top. In such cases, the writer feels that it is important to put the readers into the sweep of events, or to get them close to the main characters, as the way to entice. The crucial points of view, as in the most deft of nonfiction narratives, can be made along the route.

In a piece called "The Short, Unhappy Life of Dale-Lyn Crenshaw," Joel investigated the life of a child who lived only ten months but whose circumstance spoke volumes about state care for children at risk.

The beginning of the piece brought the readers directly into the circumstances surrounding the child's death—the false picture the parents had presented to authorities and the fact that the baby, as young as she was, had been a client of a state agent charged with her care, an agency designed to help children in trouble.

> She'd had an uncommon number of minor injuries: on her nose, a scrape; on her wrist, a pinch mark, or what looked to be one; on her groin, a mysterious bruise. The broken arm she suffered when she was seven weeks old had been the last straw. When her grandmother, aunt and uncle, and the other adults who cared for her saw her in a cast that wrapped her torso from belly to shoulder, they called the Manchester police and DCYS, the Department of Children and Youth Services. They said they feared for Dale-Lyn's life.

Joel went on to explain that DCYS then decided that despite the risk of abuse, the baby was better off with the parents; the decision was reflective of the trend toward keeping families together if at all possible instead of resorting to foster care. Joel, at that point, was beginning to hint at the real reason for the piece: a controversial policy.

Then, when the readers were sufficiently drawn into the case itself because they began to identify with the baby, Joel paused for just a paragraph to indicate the significance of the case and the point that he promised to prove:

> Obviously, DCYS made a mistake; Dale-Lyn's death proved that. But it is another thing to ask whether the mistake was excusable; to ask whether the agency did all it could to protect Dale-Lyn. . . .
> [DCYS] is a bureaucracy that as a guardian of endangered children is inherently feeble.

Following this central argument was the detail that allowed Joel to speak with such authority: the complete account of the ten months of the life of Dale-Lyn Crenshaw, intimate details of family life that had been hidden away in secret files but uncovered by a tenacious and careful reporter.

When Joel Lang talks about such writing, he speaks slowly and carefully—just as in his writing, his explanations are self-edited, precise.

"You always try to tell a story chronologically. So you've already answered one question. A question of structure.

"One of the things I constantly remind myself is to be as specific as possible, precise as possible, without letting that precision bog things down. Any time you write a cliché—not what really happened—stop yourself, and go back and try to write it some other way.

"Try to write it the way it really happened."

ஃ 6 ௸

Anatomy of a Narrative

Winning Techniques in a Case of Social Injustice

The first time David Morse ever wrote a nonfiction narrative he won two national awards and spurred social change. Yet such recognition and accomplishment could speak neither for the satisfaction of his work nor for the pain of it. For even now, when the subject of Marta Ho comes up, David cannot be un-emotional; he cannot talk about the reporting and writing of the piece and its unthinkable aftermath without his emotions showing. And without some doubts.

David had once done a researching and writing project for the University of Connecticut, the preeminent public university in the state, and his wife, Anne Joffe, is a professor of English there. So he knew the school's history and the enormous service it has provided. This made the troubles all the more difficult to accept and understand.

There had been voluminous newspaper reports about an ugly incident. Several Asian-American students had been spat upon while riding a bus to a school dance, and those students had suffered even more graphic and obscene insults at the dance itself. Further, that night seemed to be indicative of an emerging new prejudice against yet one more minority group. Many things concerned David about what was happening, not the least of which was the overt presence of bigotry on a college campus; if there is no enlightenment at institutions of higher learning where is there enlightenment? Specifically, he had

88

wondered why the white students on the bus had not defended the Asian-Americans. He wondered if two of the students accused of harassment—stars of the football team—had been accorded special treatment at the expense of others.

In short, he knew there were important stories beyond the daily headlines. "The power of the event that had happened, and my own abhorrence at the way these young people were humiliated—and the human complexity of the university response—intrigued me, plagued me, and ultimately put great demands on me as a reporter. I had done some investigative reporting, and occasionally human interest stories. I had always considered it my forte to make understandable to a mass audience relatively complex issues, but I had never tackled anything with this sort of emotional or ethical complexity." Following David through the process reveals the way to handle the most difficult reporting and writing projects.

It also turned out to be an example of "back door" writing. That is, you don't always write—or seldom write—the precise piece you set out to write. What David ultimately found— through his intense reporting and with expert guidance from Jan Winburn, *Northeast's* associate editor—was a much better story than anyone could have imagined.

"My first intention was to write about that incident. I queried *Northeast*, and drafted a rough letter to John Casteen, president of UConn, that would have told him what the article was about, and it would have asked him for an interview. I was advised by my editors at *Northeast* that the basis of the story had been told before and adequately covered in the press. They convinced me that the only way to get at the larger story—the real story of the prejudice on campus—was to focus on one student and funnel that student through a typical day. That is, to portray what it is like to be Asian-American on campus. So I attended some meetings of the student associations, interviewed several Asian and Asian-American students. Of all of them, Marta Ho was the most interesting. She was a vital person, in a way typical—even though no one was truly typical."

As David's primary editor on the piece, Jan Winburn knew that choosing the right person was critical. The key to any piece—narrative, profile, or essay—is the documentation of change; the intent is to pinpoint pertinent human forces, courage among them. Marta had seemed to show that courage. Yet our way of thinking is that good writing demands detail, that the human struggle means nothing without the subject becoming vulnerable—human, if you will. Intelligent readers are moved only when the true, sometimes unflattering picture is presented. Many writers fail to do this, sometimes because they think flaws in their heroes will mean readers won't identify with them, or because they have not put the energy necessary into the reporting. David knew he had to put that energy in, and he knew as soon as Marta opened up what a rich story it would be.

"Having picked Marta it quickly became apparent to me that the spitting incident was the central emotional fact in her life. When she talked about that night and its aftermath, she became extremely emotional; she had been traumatized. That incident, and her reaction, I knew, had to become the emotional mainspring of the piece. Obviously, the full story had not been told."

It was a much richer story than we had imagined. The events following that horrible night of the dance, most of them undocumented, appeared to speak even more forcefully about the horrors of prejudice than had the original circumstance.

So here was yet another change of plan. We decided we would not do a human interest story, we would not do a typical day in the life of an Asian-American student. We would instead reconstruct the spitting incident and its aftermath, which had been largely unreported. It was a sequence of events that would certainly demonstrate troubling truths to readers who thought the campus was a place where tolerance and administrative competency ruled.

David faced a gripping subject and daunting obstacles. A narrative was a natural way to tell what had happened, but without the whole story—that is, significant accounts from all sides—a narrative reflective of the truth would be impossible. On one side, he had reticent Asian-American students, drained by their fight against the university and unaccustomed, and to some degree unwilling, to talk to the press. On the other side was a very defensive university administration that seemed to be hiding something.

Jan advised David to hold off sending his letter to President Casteen; that it was too early to approach the authorities, that he had to have more background, more informed questions before that meeting. He might only get one opportunity to question Casteen; he needed to make it count.

Yet Marta Ho was not making it easy. She did not, at first, keep her appointments with David. She had suffered a trauma, and was not sure she wanted to live through it again for purposes of telling the story. Moreover, there was the matter of her family to consider. Her sister Maria had been a principal in the struggle, and, most significant, her father was a private and proud man who thought his daughters had brought disgrace to the family with all the attention they were getting. David said, "He was a pioneer. He brought the family to the United States. He had been professionally trained as a science teacher, and wound up working long hours in hot kitchens in countries where he couldn't speak the language. He had sacrificed a lot for his family. He was hurt by what he saw as a failure of appreciation on Marta's part."

Ultimately, she decided it was in everyone's interest to be candid—a decision made easier by David's persistence and his sensitivity in approaching Marta. While he did not go away or take no for an answer, he demonstrated his passion for the subject and his desire to record what had happened despite the obstacles, characteristics that could not help but impress his subjects. "I think she and I developed a rapport over time. I think she was trying to understand what happened to her. She wanted to communicate to other people what happened. She was struggling to be one of the crowd on one level and was painfully aware she was not going to blend. She had been wounded. We both felt that in telling the story it would be part of her healing. It could also be enabling for other people, particularly those who faced the trauma of harassment and prejudice."

He interviewed Marta Ho many times. The interviews included others on the original bus trip; that is, anyone who would speak to him. The two football players were reluctant. After many tries, one finally did. The path through the university bureaucracy was equally frustrating. The dean who had held hearings—and who had cleared the football players of wrongdoing, and in doing so had in effect accused the Asian-Americans of being the troublemakers—was not cooperative. David kept pressing. And the more he learned, the more willing everyone was to talk to him. It is generally true that in an investigative or in-depth piece (this was both), the more you know as a writer the more cooperation you will get. Sources begin to wonder what others have told the reporter, and if they will be represented fairly. They usually decide that it is in their own best interest to speak to the reporter, to put themselves in the best possible light.

And yet the interview with President Casteen, finally arranged after a substantial amount of the other reporting was done, did not go well. "I realized that one of the dimensions to the story had to be the university's full response. You couldn't do that story without dealing in an even-handed way with the institution accused of allowing racism. But when I finally talked to Casteen, it ended up a shouting match—it didn't help that he had received word that morning that the state legislature had frozen his salary. I found him cold, defensive. He thought I was ill-prepared for the interview, and that I had my mind made up."

I subsequently received a call from the university's public relations head, Anthony Brown, with his own perspective on the meeting. Clearly, the university was not pleased with how it had gone and was worried that the president would be unfairly presented. I assured Brown that our reporting had always been fair and would be fair in this case, and that whatever lack of cordiality there was between reporter and source could be addressed. In time, another interview was arranged, one that went much better, although the ground covered continued to be contested. Such moments are common when reporting stories of significance.

For David, Casteen was not the only difficult interview. For example, the state police officer to whom the incident at the dance had been first reported was largely unforthcoming and would answer questions only in the presence of several of his bosses. Perhaps that was because of the sensitivity of the questions. In her own version of the account, Marta had described to the officer in detail what happened at the dance—that one of the football players had danced with his penis exposed as a way to taunt the Asian-American women. According to one of the students, "He asked me, did I see (the football player) pull his pants down, and did I see his penis? I said I did, and he asked me, do I really know what a penis looks like?" As you may imagine, interviewing a state cop about such matters can be difficult.

The reporting was certainly demanding, and the writing was a challenge as well. David went through several revisions, each suggested by Jan, each attempting to refine the narrative, to make it precise, to include a great amount of detail, yet not too much to keep the narrative from moving forward. There was, too, the question of organization of the piece.

It was clear that the basic structure of the piece, or at least the metaphysical structure, could go from incident A to incident Z, that is, from the night of the dance to the aftermath of the investigation into it. But that was the easy part.

While it is true that a story begins at the beginning, such a truth is also simplistic. David knew that a writer must get the reader on an intimate basis with the person or people written about. No matter how important the subject—even something so critical as bigotry—the story may not deeply affect readers if they do not identify with the primary character. This generally requires human detail; such detail in this case demystifies minority group members and puts the readers in their shoes. That is, if David did his job right, he would in effect put the reader on that bus, and at the dance, and watching the football player exposing himself, and inside the administrative circus that occurred afterward. Moreover, he would document the change in his primary character—the essence of any good narrative.

David had been tremendously moved by what he had learned. He felt frustration and anxiety in considering the challenge of getting readers to the same emotional point where he found himself. "The newspaper accounts had been ordinary. The more I talked to people, the more alive the story became for me, the more it gathered substance, the more real it became, and I realized a whole lot of readers out there must have passed by the events. It goes by, with a lot of other horrors that go by, and you forget about it. These kids hadn't forgotten about it, and I wanted ordinary white people like me to understand what happened. I wanted Marta to be a real person who had suffered something awful. You wouldn't want your daughter to have something like that happen. You don't want it to happen to you."

To care about what happened to Marta Ho and to her fellow students, you first had to learn, in an economical amount of space, about Marta Ho as a human being, or else readers would not feel the full humiliation as the object of scorn and discrimination. And yet this was a hard literary dance to do. You can't spend an inordinate amount of space to get to the actual beginning of the narrative; if you do, you run the risk of losing the reader. No matter how fascinating your description of the main character, some conflict must be introduced early or, as a detective novelist would say, the gun must be placed in the upper right-hand drawer of the desk early on or the obvious drama will be missing. There are blatant and subtle ways to do this; the more literate the intention, the more subtle the approach.

Jan told David that for any author the beginning is demanding not only as an introduction of the action and characters but as a reflection, after all the reporting and thinking time, of what the writer makes of the events and circumstances. Beginnings must go beyond "clever" or "catchy"; they must capture the spirit of the reporting and establish the point of view of the piece.

Here is how David began:

> Before the dance, the word "semiformal" had the usual romantic connotations for Marta Ho—pretty dresses, corsages, crepe-paper streamers. It also suggested independence.

David saved the best in the opening paragraph for last. "Independence" is a key word in the piece, a key idea to keep the narrative moving forward.

> All through high school, Marta had struggled for accep-

tance. "I wanted to fit in so badly," she says. Her mother and father, who had emigrated from China by way of Taiwan and South America, would not let her have boyfriends or stay out late. Branford High School was overwhelmingly white, and Marta hadn't gone to dances.

"My father was trying to keep a little China around us. He knew that we were in America, but 'Don't be American. . . . Don't live that kind of lifestyle; don't start drinking; don't start smoking; don't start having boyfriends. Don't, don't, don't.' " She delivers his remarks in a singsong litany, then laughs. "I hated high school. I don't think I liked myself, either."

Marta is 22 now, a senior at the University of Connecticut. She has been an American citizen for six years. She talks in the breezy post-literate style of her college peers, the softened Chinese "r" the only sign of an accent. Forsaking syntax for verve, she regularly inserts little dialogues in midsentence to make a point. She has an expressive face, ready to laugh; hair swept back from her high forehead; hands usually fidgeting.

Critical here are two things. The "gun in the right-hand drawer" is not so simply defined. Did David put it there? The mention of the dance, which puts readers on notice that its accounting would be coming up, certainly is one example of the gun. But there is a more subtle drama as well: the conflict between father and daughter, between values. Also critical in the beginning of this narrative was David's ability to describe Marta in human terms. Marta, as we suspect, will turn out to be a hero, but she is not a one-dimensional character. Already she is described as having doubts about herself and her place in society as well as concern about the conflict over family values. The reader is necessarily left with the correct impression that in the course of the narrative many conflicts will be addressed, not only the spitting incident. Such writing begins to reflect, then, a much truer and more meaningful account of difficult times than presented in any other form of nonfiction. After describing Marta, David chooses this moment to write the nut graph. Such a paragraph, as pointed out earlier, is not always necessary, but when an investigation uncovers news or leads to a startling conclusion, strong arguments can be made for putting it near the top of the story.

> Headlines tell a bare-bones story. Eight Asian students step onto a crowded bus bound for a semiformal dance. They are spat upon repeatedly and called names. But headlines and news stories do little to show what it's like to be an Asian-American on a college campus, to be the victim of racial harassment. Nor do they reveal the reverberations and deep tremors the incident still sends through the Storrs campus, or the change in Marta Ho.

Early versions of this nut graph were much different. They were necessarily preliminary. Such a paragraph can be written correctly only when the piece is entirely reported and written, so that the points are not overstated or undersold. Nor should it include too much detail—else the story will have been told twice or, worse, the general reader, always tempted anyway to repair to the television set, will think the essentials of the story have been related and there is no point in continuing.

David then chose to prepare readers for the dance by giving a more detailed picture of Marta and her family history—the hard work, obedience, modesty inherent in family values, the fact that her older sister, Maria, was the first to rebel against their father's prohibitions against dating and makeup, and the fact that Marta was always "the new kid on the block." She said, "I always wanted to be one of those people who lived in a house with the white picket fence and friends they've known since kindergarten. Now I wouldn't exchange that for my own experience." In these descriptions David was getting very close to Marta Ho and setting up the bus scene very well.

> On the evening of December 3, 1987, at about 9:30, Marta and seven other students of Asian descent boarded a bus that was to take them to a semiformal Christmas dance sponsored by two dorms. . . . They were dressed up, Marta in a black-and-white, knee-length gown made

of silk, which she had borrowed from her sister. Her friend, Feona Lee, was wearing a full-length, blue silk gown that she had brought from her native Hong Kong. . . . It was Feona who had gotten the eight people together, setting Marta up with Lenny Chow, a senior in engineering. While Lenny was technically her date, as far as Marta was concerned they were just eight people going out to dance.

The crowded bus held between 50 and 60 people, according to Marta—some of them drinking and yelling profanities. . . .

Marta and her friends waited quietly while the bus remained parked in front of Belden Hall. Suddenly, Feona, who was sitting on someone's lap, felt something land in her hair. "At first I thought it was just water dripping from the bus. Then I felt something warm and slimy hit me in the face." She realized it was spit. As she stood and turned to face her attackers, she was hit again, this time in the eye. "Who did that?" she screamed. "Stop!"

David went on further to describe the scene, in which the two football players yelled slurs such as "Chinks!" and "Oriental faggots!" Apologies were demanded, none forthcoming, and a fight broke out that was quickly stopped. The harassment continued. A large group in the back of the bus began singing "We All Live in a Yellow Submarine," and the taunting did not stop until arrival at the Italian-American Club in Tolland, where the sexual harassment occurred. In this description, which is only outlined here, David was indeed able to put the details behind the headlines, to actually put readers on the bus, to describe the attitudes of both the perpetrators of the harassment and the victims. To do this, he had to know the particulars of the conversation, of the taunting. He had to know the lyrics of the songs. He found out not from one source—that would have been suspect—but from several: interviews with victims, police officers, and university officials; sworn affidavits in police reports; and internal university memos. David continued the narrative by describing what happened when Marta and Feona tried to get police help and found a dispute over jurisdiction and, hence, no help at all, notwithstanding the conversation Feona had with the state trooper about whether she could identify male body parts. Then David brought readers back to the present.

> Last May, 17 months later, Marta still couldn't talk about what had happened without reliving it. Her eyes welled up with tears when she tried to describe the anger and the hurt—the sense of her human rights being violated. "And nobody was going to do anything about it."

Now that the reader had invested in this story, had been led up to this horrible event in the way Marta had, David was ready to describe the heroic effort of Marta and others to find justice somewhere, an effort obviously complicated by more obedient family values. David described Maria's outrage upon hearing her sister's account and how she arranged to get Feona and Lenny Chow to go to the campus police, who claimed lack of jurisdiction in that the incident had happened off campus. Finally, Maria called the university's Office of Affirmative Action Programs and made an appointment. But it was just one more authority that employed the jurisdiction excuse. David was beginning to describe what was clearly becoming an epic struggle. Finally the students were referred to the dean of students. When arrangements were unsatisfactory, the students threatened to go to the press with their concerns. David chose this point in the narrative to pause—to give what every narrative on serious issues requires: background and perspective. Given too early, say at the beginning of the piece, this pause would turn readers off; they would not stick with the narrative. The emotional connection would be too weak. But now that the incident has been related in detail, Marta's struggle for justice had begun, and readers were on the edges of their armchairs, David could take a moment to show how this story fits into a historical and contemporary context.

> Racism was not an issue widely talked about on the UConn campus in the early 1980s. . . .

The number of Asian students had doubled between 1982 and 1987, and the isolated campus in Storrs was struggling to deal with its growing cultural diversity. The problem was by no means unique to UConn; Asian enrollment had increased at most colleges, and there was talk of "new racism" on campuses nationwide.

David went on to describe some of the steps President Casteen had taken to address the issue and some of the objective evidence that showed a difference between intention and follow-through. If righting racial harassment wrongs was on the university's agenda, it seemed clear from David's reporting that it was not at the very top of that agenda. On the other hand, the dean's office did move quickly in the case of the spitting incident. The two football players were charged with violating the student conduct code. Even so, it was a hard time for victims.

Marta went through a period of blaming herself. "I think as the victim you do that. And a lot of people did blame us. Our parents asked us, 'Did you dress funny? Did you all wear, like, gangster outfits or something? . . . Why did you have to go to the dance?' "

Once again, here is David showing the real Marta Ho, not a comic-strip hero. Now came a very critical part of the piece. David described the hearings held at the dean's office to investigate the possible role of the football players. These hearings occurred over two days, the first day's lasting until late at night in the presence of the university ombudsman, who had agreed to come as a neutral observer, and the second without him, when the hearing took a decidedly favorable turn toward the football players. The particulars of the testimony and the maneuvering are fascinating—the dean included only the male students in the second hearing—but are too lengthy to go into here. Suffice to say that the results of the hearing were relatively light punishment for the athletes and university statements that their being athletes did not inspire special treatment. David then summarized the reaction of the Asian-American students and their opinion that the administrators' treatment of them was as bad as the original incident, or worse. He then described the next step in their plan: calling in experts on addressing bigotry, among them Peter Kiang. This event allowed David to include more critical background on the subject.

> Kiang debunks the "myth of the model minority"—the stereotype of Asian-Americans as successful, hardworking, obedient, and uncomplaining. The danger of the myth . . . is that it is used to manipulate Asians and other minorities as well as the public at large. On the surface, it appears positive—preferable to the older stereotypes of Asians as laundry workers or coolie laborers. But a look at its history shows that the model minority image, promoted heavily in the national media in the 1960s, during riots in Watts and Detroit, and again in the 1970s and early 1980s, was used by some to undermine affirmative action programs. It sent a message to the blacks . . . to say, 'Why can't you be like the Asians?' . . . [It was] a way of disciplining blacks in their demands for social equality. . . .
>
> Kiang observed that on the one hand the myth of the model minority is "praising Asian-Americans for 'making it.'" On the other hand it can also be interpreted as a warning: "Watch out for the Asians; they're taking over."

Again, including such perspective and interpretation is essential to any meaningful narrative. Far from slowing down the events, they only serve to make the reader feel more deeply toward the subject matter. David then described how Marta and Maria began to organize, running meetings for fellow Asian-American students. David wrote, "Together, they began to chip away at what they saw as a wall of indifference. . . . They wanted to press for concrete changes." Even so, David found complications.

> Maria complained of feeling "burnt out." Marta was feeling like an errand girl for Maria. The organization of

Asian-American students they had founded was already divided between those who wanted to continue to pursue a "political" course and those who feared the group's activism would only isolate them further from the mainstream campus. . . .

Ultimately David describes the encouraging campus response to the struggle of the Ho sisters and the change in attitude of President Casteen upon meeting Marta and Maria. "Their first-hand reports were much more affecting. . . . I realized the trauma they had undergone. . . ." It is quite likely that readers knew more about Marta Ho and her companions than President Casteen did prior to that time. The eventual result of the campaign by the Ho sisters was the appointment of a special committee that recommended significant changes in university policy. David documented these results as well as the fact that such awareness and change had other ironic consequences, such as the expulsion of an Asian-American student for putting a sign on her door that was offensive to homosexuals. The piece as a whole offered more than irony to readers: that racism, as much as any subject of significance, is seldom clearly defined. David quoted one observer that, in matters of accountability for such incidents, "We are all complicit, every one of us. Institutionalized racism is rarely overt. It takes the form of resistance, lack of support, inertia, inactivity." David saved the last section of the piece for his protagonist.

Marta seems unable, for now, to put the incident aside. There is a part of her that has not yet healed. Her voice rises whenever she talks about what happened that night—especially when she describes how other Asians implied that she did something wrong. . . . In her quieter moments, she talks about the positive changes that have taken place in the past two years. She has become more assertive, more conscious of her identity as an Asian-American. . . .

She went through a period of "reverse discrimination," of looking down on whites. "I was over-proud of myself. I was over-proud of our accomplishments, of my culture. I thought that we were superior. . . . And when I catch myself I realize that I'm going through a problem stage. . . . I was beginning to think and talk like my father!" . . .

Over her father's protests, Marta has switched her major from math—which she has always found easy—to the humanities, where she has to struggle, especially with English. Somewhere in that choice, she supposes she may be fighting what she calls the "stereotype of Asians as big super-achievers and technocrats." . . .

What advice does she have for Asian-Americans starting college? "Don't deny your ethnicity. Don't be a banana or a Twinkie (someone who is Asian on the outside, but white inside). You've got to like yourself. Your hair, your flat nose, slanted eyes. If you don't like yourself, I don't think anybody else will. . . . And if you think your rights are being violated, do something about it; don't just complain. That's what Asians do all the time; we sit around and complain. You know, if you want some difference, make the difference."

The very last part of the piece—where such news is most effective in a narrative—reported that Marta and Maria were recipients of an award from the UConn Women's Studies program for work "reflecting a dedication to the understanding and advancement of minority women in the U.S." By having invested in the difficulties and the energies of the Ho sisters, the reader, in effect, received the award as well. The reader appreciates it much more now than if it had been mentioned earlier. David ended the piece:

Marta's father attended the ceremony, wearing a dark suit and a red shirt. He was beaming.

Such a narrative lies at the heart of what has compelled me to continue working in Sunday magazines. There can be no more important stories than those that inspire social change—and this one certainly did. Hundreds of thousands of readers and a university administration now thought differently about matters of prejudice because David Morse brought its ugliness home through a riveting narrative.

David's piece was also acknowledged in distinguished writing circles. He received the Unity Award for reporting on minority issues and was a winner in the annual competition of Sunday magazines for investigative and in-depth reporting.

And yet the acknowledgment and accomplishment do not at this point overcome the news received the very spring that the awards were received. Marta Ho's father—still harboring doubts about his daughter's way of life and still, despite his attendance at the award ceremony, incommunicative with his daughter—was killed when a drunk driver hit his car. David Morse wonders if his piece may have further alienated father and daughter. But there are other pertinent questions. How much did David Morse contribute to explaining and illuminating a crucial issue? How well did he document the courage and contributions of an extraordinary young woman? These questions have positive answers. For in the end, David Morse did all that a good writer can do.

༄ 7 ༄

Courage in Profiles

Testing Your Ability in Inevitability

A glance at the neighborhood newsstand is evidence enough of the popularity of the profile. Most consumer magazines—even those such as *Vanity Fair* that offer unorthodox literary adventure—reserve their covers for pretty faces. For discerning readers, this is a dreary state of affairs; there is hardly a way to distinguish one magazine from another. But for you as a writer, this practice signals a world of opportunity. Editors of consumer magazines know that in the matter of newsstand sales, the quality material on the inside is of secondary consideration to the cover. It is the cover that sells, and nothing sells as well as a hot personality. This is often the case in a Sunday magazine, even if its welfare does not rely on newsstand success; the challenge here is to entice readers from the competition—the other sections of its own paper.

There is no larger literary market than the profile market. And to further underscore its attractiveness to you, note that the majority of profile subjects are willing ones: they have something to sell—a new book or movie, for example. It is in their interest to make themselves available.

The art of the profile, then, is critical to you as a writer. Yet in many ways it can be the trickiest form of nonfiction. It requires getting close to the subject, and yet also maintaining a distant and thoughtful perspective. It often plumbs areas the subject wishes were not examined. There is the rather enormous presumption of making sense—or a theme—out of another person's life. And there is the unscientific matter of structure, which does not necessarily suggest itself the way it does in a personal essay or narrative. Few profiles in general interest magazines can begin at birth. It is easy, for example, to spot a profile in which the point of view is undeveloped: the return to formative years comes too early in the piece. As readers, we must first have a sense of a contemporary crisis—that is, a change or challenge in the subject's life—before our curiosity compels us to investigate origins.

This is not to paint a forbidding picture, only to point out that there are good reasons to undertake profiles and certain difficulties common to most. It may be easy enough to settle on a subject; that is, someone who is emerging in business or entertainment or politics. It is quite another job to dig to that person's roots, not merely family roots, but spiritual roots, because in the end a profile is in many ways just like any other serious piece of writing: it depends for its success on story telling, on the writer's eye for significant detail, and on the writer's point of view.

In the largely subjective matters of writing and editing, I subscribe to the principle of inevitability. A simpler phrase for it might be "good timing," but inevitability, as you will see, is much more than that. An inevitable piece is one that is crying out to be done. This is an article that readers find timely and irresistible, as if they say to themselves, "I've been wanting to read about this. Thank goodness this is here." However, in each community, in each publication, the matter of inevitability is defined differently. You must know your market. You must anticipate the needs of the publication.

Consider what was, for example, inevitable in Miami. Over the years there, it seemed logical to explore critical contemporary moments in the lives of many famous Florida residents such as Jackie Gleason, Robert Rauschenberg, and Tennessee Williams. In a sense, such personalities helped define the place in which all of us lived. Gleason, for example, was ebullient about south Florida, a one-man chamber of commerce. But an inevitable picture of another comedian, a man that fewer people had heard of, speaks more to the point here.

The idea struck both Michael Winerip and me long before he became a *New York Times* columnist. As residents of south Florida, we both knew about the phenomenon of the "condo comics," men who were children of vaudeville and, in their retirements, could now make a buck playing at senior citizen complexes on Saturday nights. It was a piece, Michael knew, that could get to the heart of the community because it would not only profile one colorful entertainer but also explore subjects endemic to the area. Consequences of the aging process, for example, make for more compelling reading in south Florida than in other regions because it is a retirement haven. In short, the condo comic was an inevitable story.

An excerpt from the piece examines both the philosophy of the subject, Guy Rennie, and the character of retirement communities. It begins with comedian Rennie's account of schmoozing the people who had hired him for the night, people who once may have had positions of responsibility in society and now must take their satisfactions where they may.

> First thing you have to do at the condo, he'd say, is corner the entertainment committee before the show. "You tell them a dirty joke. You say I know I can't tell this tonight, but you'll enjoy it. They like that. They feel important. . . .
>
> "So you kibitz (in the actual performance) a little bit. A guy has on red pants, you say, 'I bet you didn't dress like that in Brooklyn.' They can be as old as hell—they can be the oldest audience I've ever seen and I always flatter them. I'll say, 'This is the youngest crowd I've seen all week.' They laugh. . . .
>
> "At the end the committee will usually yell, 'Tell the dirty joke, tell the dirty joke. The one you told us before the show.' [That night] I told the dirty joke. Three old women in the first row—I swear—peed in their pants."

In just a few words, the reader learns not only the philosophy of the comic, but something about the aging process, the comforts of nostalgia, and of an audience giving itself license to laugh.

The principle of inevitability is certainly the major rule of the profile. This requires that you understand the nature of your community, that you stay abreast of the news and of trends, and that you test your instincts. How do you know what profile will be interesting to readers? How do you know what will be an inevitable piece? The first test is whether the subject you propose intrigues you. There is no getting around this. That sense of inevitability, of excitement, that must several weeks or months later be passed on to the reader, is not possible unless it exists in the mind of the writer.

Many times a novice writer will ask me, "Do you have any assignments—any profiles you want me to write?" The answer usually disappoints—because I'm looking for more than just the willingness to invest weeks of time into the interpretation of a subject's life. I am looking for fire, for a compelling reason to undertake a difficult form.

Here are some key circumstances that persuade me to invest time and energy in a profile: the writer's desire, the timeliness of the subject of the profile—that is, will that person be in the news when the piece appears?—and whether that writer may be able to give that portrait an edge. There is little point in a profile that simply regurgitates a life's work. The best profiles, just like the best fiction and nonfiction narratives, capture a contemporary moment of change in the subject: growth, decline, risk, or experimentation. And the best of the best have access to the subject during that period.

That is not to say that all the problems are solved when the right subject is determined. There is still the matter of reporting, getting the subject to speak candidly, settling on something illuminating to say about the subject, how the piece will be shaped, and what tone will emerge. All of these considerations faced Gary Dorsey when he undertook a potentially explosive project at *Northeast*.

J. W. Farrands was a worker in a razor factory in the town of Shelton, Connecticut, who achieved a controversial distinction. He was the first northerner, and first Catholic, elected as Imperial Wizard of the Ku Klux Klan.

The decision to profile Farrands was easy to make, yet I

confess I entrusted the piece only to a staff writer on the magazine because of some obvious risks. Traditionally, newspapers show ambivalence to such characters. Although they are "news," there is concern that ordinary coverage serves only the purposes of the hate groups, not the public at large. Such an issue is not easy to resolve in the hypothetical; certainly it is possible for a publication to make too much of bigots. But as with everything else in a general interest magazine, how to fill the space is a matter of judgment, a matter of taste, a matter of deciding what will compel the reader and what will both enlighten and entertain. It has never been my view to disqualify as subjects those who demonstrate obnoxious public behavior. In fact, I tend toward the opposite view: the more we explore the forces of bigotry, the better equipped we are to understand it and effect its decline. That was the theory for pursuing the Farrands piece. Gary Dorsey, as the reporter and writer, was faced with the reality.

Reflecting on the project, Gary observed, "You always go into such a piece with preconceived ideas. And then, of course, as you learn more and more about a person, the more your preconceived ideas are destroyed. This is the point that throws you into chaos, because you don't know what you will say. You've got to figure out who the guy is. Meeting Farrands, talking to him, doing the initial interview at his home, I got some sense of it. In some ways he was a likable sort of oaf. He didn't talk like a racist."

Yet there was the undeniable fact that Farrands was now the head of an organization whose hate is inscribed into its constitution, its "Kloran." Herein lies the danger of the ordinary newspaper profile. Left only to a few hours of observation and interviews and largely reporting quotes and incidents, there is really no way to effectively capture the spirit of the subject matter. Objective evidence only goes so far in the way of revelation—it tends to present conflicting arguments, perhaps well made, but rote. It is up to the good, cautious, serious writer to make sense of such a subject as the Imperial Wizard.

"It was like a lot of stories," Gary said. "You think you know what it is, but then you wonder." The only way to move toward a better understanding, to put your finger on the precise point between likability and hate, is more research and more thinking time. Gary was able to arrange to be with Farrands on two important trips early in his term of office. It was during those trips, not during the conversations, that the portrait emerged. The key in any portrait is getting as close as possible to the person, and it was only when Farrands left the factory and the familiarity of his house—only when Gary's presence was no longer foreign—that he let his guard down and began to open up. And Gary was a good listener. "A lot of times people like to have an audience, and I'm a pretty good audience. A sage once said, 'No man is an asshole to himself.' I keep that in mind. All subjects have a point of view of their own and they've somehow rationalized it. I let them talk about their lives, their childhood experiences, and so forth. So we can see how they came to the point of view, even if the logic is twisted."

That thoughtful point of view may then be contrasted with the actual behavior of the subject as observed by the writer. To begin the piece, Gary decided on telling description:

Jim Farrands left the line at the razor factory like a rooster headed for a cockfight. Wrapped in the scent of anisette, he tongued a brittle Avanti cigar from one corner of a gap-toothed grin to the other. He paced in the cold with Emile Martin, a pint-sized man who silently pulled a gray Confederate cap over his brow. The limo driver looked puzzled. Who was this bowlegged guy in a Connecticut State Police ball cap?

"Nah, I'm not with the police," Farrands said.

If the other passengers wondered, too, when their ride began in the Howard Johnson's parking lot in Milford, Farrands made himself known soon enough. "Remember, this is not a noncontact sport," he told his bodyguard, George. By the time they passed the Greenwich exit, Emile and George had started calling him J.W. By the time they crossed the New York border, his New England accent had picked up a drawl. "The South shall rise again!" Emile cried.

Farrands and his companion unloaded their gear at LaGuardia and left behind a limousine full of people stunned silent: a black woman with her child, three men dressed for a business trip, a grim elderly couple from Fairfield County. During their brief time together, Farrands had boasted about his new order of white people. He'd offered to warm the backseat with a flammable "pocket cross." He had talked about skinning rattlesnakes and swilling moonshine, and shown off newly minted Klan trinkets. "These'll go fast," he'd said, flaunting a sign once hung in club cars on Cotton Belt train routes: WHITES ONLY.

No doubt Farrands was looking forward to his first flight South since becoming Imperial Wizard. He raced in and out of airport gift shops, comparing Klan prices and those of New York tourist knickknacks. "Look, a Dago place!" he shouted, heading toward Fiorelli's restaurant. In just two hours, the first Catholic and first Northerner ever to rule the Ku Klux Klan was going to enter the most active sector of his Invisible Empire at 600 mph. He would come from the sky. He had his blue robe. He had his membership roll. He had Emile and George.

Emile bought flight insurance and turned green during takeoff. George drained a minibottle of Jack Daniel's. Headed for Hot-lanta. Headed for trouble. . . .

By simply describing in some detail the Imperial Wizard's actions and companions, Gary had found the tone and point of view for which he had been searching. This approach revealed both the passion for hate in his subjects and the obvious emptiness of the Klan creed. Gary went on to describe the public demonstrations in Georgia, and ended his journey with the man whose title, in a fit of writerly derision and irony, had been shortened to "The Wiz." That scene was drawn in New York City, where Farrands had a racial confrontation on a talk show, a brouhaha induced by both innate feelings of bigotry and the ingestion of impressive quantities of alcohol.

And yet the writer may never be certain that a general audience, composed of so many different sensibilities, will take away from the piece the intended impressions. In the case of Farrands, the subject was wrought with difficulty and with the clear capacity of reinforcing, rather than diminishing, stereotypes. So it was certainly comforting to Gary to read the assessment of the profile by Roy Hattersley in his Press Gang column in the English magazine known for its own unabashed views, *Punch Weekly*:

> I calculate that over fifteen thousand words and half a dozen pictures are devoted to 'Travels with JW.' . . . Both the pictures and the prose succeed in making the Grand Wizard seem tawdry rather than terrible and his followers not so much sinister as silly. Of course, the notice "Whites Only," put up in the window of a hired New York limousine, is a cause for proper moral indignation. But when the driver is asked to take JW to Howard Beach for a pizza, the prospect of the fiery cross lighting up the midnight sky seems less terrible.

Gary himself said the approach to the piece came to him not while he was doing the interviews or on the trips but at the word processor. "You can't really figure it out until the writing process begins. You almost have to write it to find out what it really was, what it really meant. A lot of times, your preconceived ideas will slip into your copy. But then you say to yourself, well, this is not right. This is not true. And you begin to tear it down. You begin to see the real story."

Whether or not an astute reader agrees with Gary's premise— that these Klansmen are basically harmless—is a different issue. At the very least, readers can see clearly how the writer drew his conclusions: they came, for the most part, through observation, dialogue, detail. Noticing. Recording. Thinking. Feeling. Gary was not after the "universal truth" of J. W. Farrands, whatever that may have been. He was only after his own truth about Farrands. Such an undertaking was serious, and it required that the writer put himself on the line.

If the principle of encouraging the writer to develop a singular point of view based on solid reporting is followed, any subject may be undertaken. I confess that if a less serious writer than Joel Lang had proposed a profile on Busty Heart, a dancer and stripper, I would have been cool to the idea. But I knew that Joel could tell the reader not only the particulars of Busty's story but the "why" of the piece. He could make something socially redeeming out of what could easily be seen as prurient interest. The fact that in a general interest magazine some readers will fail to be persuaded should not be a deterrent if a deft touch is employed. Busty Heart was a legitimate—in Hartford, inevitable—subject. He had to find a way to explain why to a respectable readership.

His first draft of the piece did not do so until well into the middle. It began with the first time he saw Busty Heart "dance," and a description of bizarre anatomical forces. Even though it was done tastefully and with Joel's characteristic and stylish understatement, it was not right for a general audience, a great percentage of which would have to be persuaded as to the redeeming nature of the piece.

Joel realized there was a special burden on this particular beginning. Although all profiles are charged with enticing readers, this one had not only to entice but also to reveal a strong reason for undertaking such a questionable project; that is, the sense of inevitability had to be more of a physical presence than is normally the case in profiles. His final draft started with a description of the remarkable commotion Busty Heart causes whenever she appears in public. Here is an excerpt from a scene in the stands at a hockey game.

> Miss Heart was hidden from view, and once out in the concession corridor, the pod that marked her location grew to a mob. Men and teenagers pushed and shoved to get close to her. She was signing "Busty" to anything thrust toward her. Paper wasn't needed. Hands, shirtcuffs, jersey fronts—she signed them all.
>
> On the outer edge of the mob, a man held his young

son on his shoulders for a better view of whatever was happening at its center. Ten-year-old boys bounced off the human wall, unable to penetrate to see what all the excitement was about. If Miss Heart moved, the mob moved. In the eddies at the edge, women shook their heads. "Pigs," muttered a short-haired woman in a Whalers jacket. "Pigs," said her companion, almost a twin, louder. A young woman holding her male companion's sleeve said, amused, embarrassed, disapproving, "Oh, it's *that* woman." Her companion said, "Who?" and answered his own question, "Busty Heart," as if the name explained everything. . . .

Through this description of the Busty Heart phenomenon at a hockey game, Joel had gone a long way to establish the reason for the piece—Busty Heart was the object of great curiosity. Certainly that was so among sports fans and, Joel presumed, among the public at large. But if it is true that any subject can be written about—even the subject of women's breasts, by a male writer—it is all in the doing. Joel's description went a long way to justify, but where would he go now? He needed to stop, to tell people directly:

There is a very simple explanation for what happened at the Civic Center that night. Miss Heart is young, pretty, and endowed with very, very large breasts. For them, the black top she wore was no more than a saucy hammock. They are so large that people tend to react to her as if she were a gorgeous freak, or, if they happened to be men for whom no breast can be too large, as if she were a fantasy incarnate.

But there is more to the Busty Heart phenomenon than extraordinary anatomical fact. Miss Heart has chosen to make a business of her bosom, and in the last three years she has acquired such a reputation that just her name or the knowledge of her presence causes a reaction.

Well, if that reasoning process doesn't explain why the story cried out to be done, it came pretty close. And it does demonstrate that the execution of a profile is a more critical matter than the subject itself. In the hands of a writer who did not have preference for sober tone, or for understatement, such a piece could have been disastrous.

Joel's ability to establish the reason for a piece early on was critical. It is not so much a list of accomplishments or of objective evidence that gets readers interested in a person's life. It is close-up description. It is making the person real. It is the idea of setting up, in a very subtle way, that the piece will explore telling moments in the subject's life. Such an exploration must be obvious from the beginning. Here, for example, is how Robin Finn began a *Northeast* profile of Glenn Close in 1984 when the actress was starring in *The Real Thing*:

> Thirty minutes to curtain and the taxis, like a flock of yellow homing pigeons, are zeroing in on Broadway. Fifteen minutes to curtain, on the kickoff night of a second sold-out month for this lucky cast, and backstage an extremely distraught leading lady is crying her makeup into a soggy mess and yelling in the general direction of her patient leading man. Glenn Close, the native (twelve generations worth) of Greenwich, Connecticut, who caught fame and an Oscar nomination last year for her film debut in *The World According to Garp*, isn't really angry at Jeremy Irons. Instead, she's been eclipsed by a case of jitters brought on by a surprise visit from Mike Nichols, the show's director, the night before. "Unbeknownst to any of us, Mike snuck in to see the show," she explains later, "and caught us on every single unconscious little change we've added to what we're supposed to be doing." And he left a sheaf of critical notes for his actors, just a small reminder that public acclaim is no signal for them to settle too comfortably into their roles.

What this opening had was imminence, detail, conflict—and some sense of the very human, vulnerable side of the subject's

profile. By juxtaposing in a sentence the idea of great success
(sold-out houses) and a soggy makeup mess, the writer introduced us to the high-profile and emotional world of acting,
brought us there, and made us curious to explore the primary
question of the day: who is Glenn Close?

There was a profile that, as most should, began in the here
and now. Yet it would be wrong to say, despite my argument
about formative years not coming too close to the beginning,
that such a rule may never be broken. If the profile is of a
seventeen-year-old, dubbed by our magazine as the Best Basketball Player in Connecticut, it makes sense to go backward just a
few moments in time. Robin Finn began this way:

> Back when the rest of the kids were spooning down
> their Wheaties and milk with their sights set on Saturday
> morning cartoons, Tracy Lis, her blue eyes fixed, her
> coltish jaw clenched with determination, evened up the
> toes of scuffed sneakers with the white lines her dad had
> painted on the macadam driveway, and, with the me-
> thodical grace of a production-line veteran, endlessly
> pumped a chestnut-brown basketball into a hoop hung
> with string that fluttered far above her head. In a frame
> frozen into memory by a family home movie, there she
> stands, nine years old, glaring at her target, her breath
> pluming out around her, her oversized hands, gloveless
> despite the cold, familiarly cradling the ball that, she
> seemed to intuit even then, held her future, her chance
> of one day gracing the front of that cereal box. Some
> days Tracy, undaunted by distraction, would stand out-
> side for hours on end in the worshipful pose of an
> athlete poised to bridge the gap between effort and
> achievement, perfecting her free throw, her outside shot,
> her fleet lay-up. Some days she would balk at the pros-
> pect of heaving the ball hundreds of times at the same
> unmoving receptacle, and on those days, silently, her
> grandfather would leave the house, trudge out to the
> driveway, and begin taking those practice shots himself.
> He was never out there alone for long.

Such a beginning had several advantages. Although Tracy Lis was a famous name in the sports pages, it is fair to say she was not a household name where sports pages were seldom turned to. Starting the piece with her objective accomplishments— points scored, rebounds—would risk presenting the idea this was just a "jock" story. But any good profile is a person story; it is the study of a man or woman against the world, in many cases, the story of triumph. The more detail a writer can give it, the more sense of the human quality, the better. This is not to say that the writer should exaggerate the achievement; the achievement should stand on its own. In the case of Tracy Lis, Robin was clearly able to say to the reader right away that this young woman was worth reading about. She returned to a critical moment. It was easy to picture the nine-year-old child on the court, in the cold, alone. And, at the same time, the reader sets up an expectation, a hope, that the child will succeed. That is, Robin found a way to get the reader, even the nonsports reader, into the life of Tracy Lis, so that by the time the objective measures and the particulars of basketball arrive in the piece, readers are ready for them in a way they would not be if it were presented simply as a way to write about sports.

Despite what may be viewed as narrow interests of readers, most really do have a tolerance for new subjects, for learning. The challenge to the writer is simply to make the reader care enough to explore a subject that may be off-putting. For example, if you were to ask general interest readers to embark on an eight thousand-word study of the French horn, you would have a hard sell on your hands. If, however, you found a way, as Alan Sternberg once did, of making the French horn (or more specifically, the French horn player) a very human story, the reader will follow the writer anywhere, even into fairly deep discussions on the nature of Johannes Brahms's darkest moods.

Sternberg, now a regular contributor to *The New Yorker*, wrote a profile for *Northeast* in 1982 that is a study in how a profile ought to be done. It explained a difficult subject. It was personal. It had imminence, it detailed a moment of change and risk in a person's life, and the structure was perfect, setting up the problem—the tension—and taking the reader through it.

Sternberg began with the news that Joel Winter, French horn player, would make his Lincoln Center solo debut—if only a thirty-second solo (a mere fourteen notes)—in a matter of a month. The half-minute on stage, as Sternberg explained, would represent a lifetime of preparation. Moreover, there was this:

> Eight years before, [Winter] had been about as down and out as a classical musician could get. Torn from his instrument, he was working in a print shop in the basement of Waterbury Hospital.

Having set up some tension in the piece, having planted in the reader's mind some sense of Joel Winter—a French horn player, to be sure, but a human being who faced a challenge—Sternberg was now able to continue his exposition. He explained:

> The French horn . . . is the most recalcitrant of beasts. It isn't like a piano, on which you may press a key and be reasonably sure a certain note will come out. The French horn, for any number of mystical reasons, could suddenly abandon its melancholy sweetness and moo like a sick cow, squawk like a crow, or imitate the intestinal rumblings of an elephant. . . .

Such problems affect all French horn players, but the significant complication for Winter was later explained:

> Something went wrong with his lips. Occasionally, at the worst possible times, they would begin to tremble and he would lose control of them. The formation of the lips required for playing the French horn and other wind instruments is a complicated thing involving over 200 muscles in the face and neck. It is called embouchure. Winter's seemed possessed by demons. When it began to break down, his lips would wobble around in the mouthpiece, lose their delicate interplay with each other, and cut off the sound in mid-passage. There were several disasters during symphony performances, incidents that

would have given many classical musicians nervous breakdowns. He couldn't work under these circumstances, Winter soon realized. It was like trying to play fullback with a broken leg.

Winter consulted a physician, then a psychiatrist. Neither helped. His colleagues were horrified for him. The foundations of his life—his source of income, 16 years of education and effort, all his self-esteem—were crumbling. Winter said, "I was terrified to pick the horn up; I knew what was going to happen. Sometimes it was like a muscle spasm; my mouth would rip right out of the mouthpiece."

In effect, the writer was making a promise to the reader—he was promising thirty seconds of destiny. It would be thirty seconds in one of the world's most distinguished concert halls to see if Joel Winter could make it through the fourteen notes of the bell solo in the midst of Brahms's First Symphony. Such a promise is compelling, and buys the writer time to illuminate what is for many a very dense topic.

We learn about Brahms: "It took him twenty years to write his First Symphony. He was haunted by the ghost of Beethoven." We learn how Winter felt after his breakdown:

> I don't think anyone can describe the misery. It was a tidal change in lifestyle, a fall from self-respect to worthlessness. I couldn't perform, and I had no other skills. The problems of my indulgence in self-pity were only topped by the fact that I had a one-year-old child to support and a wife who couldn't work because she had to take care of the infant. . . . When I got maudlin, I'd think that the horn was the one thing that made me special, that made me worth something and I'd lost it. . . .

We learned what he did to try to recover, and eventually were taken through the treatment of one Carmine Caruso, "a guru of sorts for brass players," who prescribed a new setting for Winter's lips. Even so, recovery was spotty.

This is not to say that the writer filled the piece with contrived tension; he merely told the story as he had seen it. He took the reader through selected moments at rehearsals, and was able to weave into the narrative specifics about classical performance that by themselves might elude most indifferent readers but in the context of a human story served to make the piece even more effective, the tension even greater.

Finally, the night of the performance, Winter was described pacing downstairs, listening to the Prokofiev, the first part of the program, as it came through the white-walled catacombs under the stage.

> "What happens, happens," he said. Then he lifted the horn and pumped out several exploratory blats. . . .
> Winter was sweating. He was quivering. In the back of his mind was the unspeakable thought: What if *it* happened again? At Lincoln Center? As the solo approached, it was as if he were being buffeted by winds.

Then there was this key sentence, drawn from an hour later, describing the musician's own account of what happened that night on stage, as the writer coaxed from his subject his strategy, the key to the Winter recovery:

> "There's a definite aspect of cliff jumping to it, and at the last minute I just said, 'Go for it. The hell with this. I'm taking every chance I can. The hell with the risks.' There is a timpani roll just before the solo, and I remember it was my last thought. When you're flying through the air, you're not thinking. After the solo was over I was so involved with the piece, so deep into the game, that my mind was a sort of blank. I didn't really know how well I'd done until everything was over."

The triumphant scene was described, the clear bell notes, the enthusiastic audience reaction, Winter being asked to stand by the conductor. And then, a lovely ending to the piece, a scene in the lobby where we meet Winter's mother, seemingly oblivious to the entire tension of the night, who says simply, "Tonight I saw my son play in Lincoln Center."

இ௯ ௯

When you arrange the sort of accessibility that Alan Sternberg arranged, you obviously gain a distinct advantage; the story, to a large degree, unfolds before you. Such access, of course, is not always possible.

In fact, the more celebrated the personality, the less access you will get. Even when they are approached in a timely fashion—that is, when they have something to sell—they will set aside an hour for you. Hardly enough to do much beyond a superficial song and dance. Getting celebrities to sit for you is a difficult business but with sufficient energy and wits a writer can do much better than early indications would indicate. When you are dealing with luminaries, you are dealing with large egos, people who, despite their arguments about cramped schedules, yearn for attention. The first thing to remember is to take what they give you. Don't be discouraged if someone advises you, as Hume Cronyn advised writer Bob Sudyk, that you can come to the house if you want but there won't be much time.

On the surface, Cronyn and his wife, Jessica Tandy, would seem to have little patience for local reporters. National publicity may be helpful, but letting neighbors read about intimate life details may encourage problems at home. Celebrities do not want fans invading their private property. And yet, Bob Sudyk had something to offer this famous acting couple. An ear.

They had a cause—aging with dignity at home. It was a real-life story whose theme had an uncanny resemblance to that of *Driving Miss Daisy,* for which Miss Tandy had won an Oscar the previous year, 1989. In their real lives, the couple was very concerned about the future and about being able to stay in their home during the inevitable infirmities of old age. To make that possible, they wanted to construct an apartment over the garage for live-in help. Permission had to be sought from their town's zoning board, and a hearing was arranged.

Bob Sudyk went to the hearing and was surprised, as most of the observers were, when the board refused to allow the permit. Such a ruling, however, left Tandy and Cronyn uncommonly accessible. Having shown up at the hearing, Bob had established a credential with his subjects. He could pick up the phone, as he did the next day, and arrange an interview, even if the time allowed would seem inadequate. The point is to take anything you are given. Once you are in their living room, as Bob was a few days later, once you listen attentively, as Bob did, and once you demonstrate to your subjects your impressive research into their lives, as Bob certainly did, the results are almost always more rewarding than anticipated. These distinguished actors told Bob about very personal things, including their distinct fears about aging.

Remember, they had something to sell—a political point of view—which is why they made themselves available in the first place. The unburdening of their souls, however, occurred because Bob had done his homework and was a keen listener. And he was not discouraged by what appeared to be limited access.

As it turned out, a second hearing was held, and the actors obtained their permit—the result was revealed in the epilogue of a very affecting piece.

Keen interest in the subject matter often yields results. When Maddy Blais wanted to profile Tennessee Williams in Key West—an idea suggested by ugly news events on the island when bigots mugged and beat up members of the homosexual community, including Williams—he was cool, even unresponsive. Maddy made it a point to send him samples of her work. Some of these samples were profiles, and all of the profiles were complex. They were not puff pieces; they showed depth and sensitivity as well as style. She also wrote him letters. She did not promise a point of view he would necessarily share, but the quality and thought of the letters were persuasive; Williams could see how important he and his troubled circumstances were to Maddy. Even so, the best he would offer was an hour or two. Maddy asked me whether I could invest some serious travel money in something that might not pan out. The answer was yes, and it was a yes that was based on Maddy's instinct as a writer. She felt she had made some connection with Williams, and that there was a decent chance he would give her more time. And so it happened. Maddy spent four days in Key West, much of the time with the playwright. She spent time at his house, with his friends, and about town. She came back with a gripping piece—cover lines are always better when the profile is brilliant. These particular lines were drawn directly from Maddy's piece:

> On January 5, his gardener was murdered. Since then, this man has twice been attacked on the streets of Key West, where he has lived for 30 years. One evening, some children gathered at his doorstep and yelled, at America's greatest playwright, "Come on out, faggot!" It reads like a play: the theme, mindless cruelty. But Tennessee Williams isn't likely to write it. He's living it.

Anne Longley often writes about celebrities for *Northeast*. She was able to get the first magazine interview with Andy Rooney after the CBS commentator was suspended for racist and homophobic remarks.

Although she will write letters and send samples of her work, her favorite technique is simply to pick up the phone. That's how she arranged the Rooney piece.

She used the phone to gather material as well. As in any serious profile, the views of friends and foes are critical: they give the piece both the edge and the perspective it requires. Anne says, "I did a lot of legwork and interviewed many people. Without Walter Cronkite, Homer Bigart, or Douglas Edwards, the piece would have been one-dimensional. With those interviews, you get a view of the century you would never have gotten otherwise."

What does she say when she calls? "First, I have a lot of

contacts from people I've known over the years. When I call, I just act like myself. I'm unpretentious. I say, 'Hi, Mr. Cronkite. I write for *Northeast* magazine in Hartford and I'm doing a piece on Andy Rooney, and I know you guys were war buddies and I'd like your comments.' That sets up a scenario for them. I also like to mention something we have in common, like a friend in Nantucket. Then they relax. There's something in the tone of your voice and how you approach people with some confidence that gets them to talk."

In person with Rooney, Anne found the commentator resistant at first. "But I just dealt with him fair and square. I didn't pretend I was somebody I wasn't. It just wouldn't have been me. [Early in the conversation, she even revealed that she had never attended college.] If I try to appear like some sophisticated writer from *The New Yorker*, it wouldn't work. I get my best stories when they think of me just as if I were a nonwriter, just another person. We talk about idle stuff. It is mainly a sense of trust, a sense they get that they can say anything. They don't think I'm out to get them."

Anne's lack of "credentials" does not dissuade her from calling the most intimidating of subjects. She thought nothing, for example, of ringing up Henry Kissinger and asking him for some time for a profile, a request that he granted her but not others. How does she do it? Positive thinking, research, and being her natural, inquisitive, charming self.

Of course, once you get your subject to sit for you, you are in a sense both writer and painter; it is your job to put the reader in your chair, to see what you see, to feel what you feel. Consider how well, for example, writer Charles Buffum did those things in describing for *Northeast* the ornery New York radio personality, Don Imus:

Imus has a cowboy face, lined and weathered, framed by a runaway mop of curly hair. The eyes are *not* kind. They burn from under thick, arched brows, the kind of eyes that undress women and size up men on the basis of whether the creep can hurt me or not. Yet, they are intelligent eyes, very human; eyes that must have seen a lot of back streets and brown bag lunches, hungry nights and fat paychecks; eyes that missed a couple of sucker punches at times, but are determined not to let *that* happen again.

ᘓ ᘙ

The goal of any profile writer ought to be to illuminate not only the general readership but those who know the subject intimately, even those who may have disdain for the subject. For that reason, every source must be plumbed, even those who are hostile to the subject.

One of the traps of the profile is that the more a writer gets to know the subject, the more affection there is, the more possibility that the subject assumes that the piece will contain nothing troublesome.

Such assurance is not always possible, of course. Any meaningful, truthful piece will touch upon character flaws. And certainly the most successful people are often the ones with no shortage of enemies—some who feel they may have been wronged and some who are envious of the subject's success. It is up to the profile writer, first, to uncover these objections to the person profiled, and then select the substantive ones for investigation and confrontation. The ultimate intention should be to complete a profile that is on the one hand neither gratuitously offensive to the subject nor on the other naive or dull. Perhaps it is overstating the case to say that every possible profile subject has detractors, but I don't think so. And, depending on the gravity of the subject matter, a writer must decide how much of it merits attention and at what point to confront his or her subject with it.

That is, the profile of an actor or actress does not necessarily suggest going out to find what other actors think of that person. But any negative reviews might be pertinent. If the subject is a real estate developer—someone bound to have made enemies in neighborhoods, among politicians, or among other developers—there is a more fertile area to explore. And there is more chance for land mines. The writer, in the end, is the one who must determine the suitability of including unfavorable information. And the writer must decide when to interview these sources and when to present the substance of those interviews to the subject. It is always a question of "when" and not one of "if." No negative charges in profiles, or any other piece, should appear about primary subjects or peripheral ones without the opportunity for rebuttal.

ﬆ ﬅ

The best solution is for the writer to establish some kind of initial relationship with the subject. The first step—even before the person is contacted—is initial research. The more you know about the subject, the more interest you show in his or her life, the less likely your request for time will be turned down. Then, in the first meeting, it is wise to cover noncontroversial areas. The writer might ask the subject about childhood and about accomplishments. Any hard questions might be saved for later. The idea is to establish rapport. This is not to say a writer should mislead the subject by saying that nothing but favorable information will be included, only that the writer and the subject get to know each other as people, in the way that Anne Longley suggests. Between interviews is the time to gather information from some of the more hostile sources. If those conversations are held too soon, the subject may get the impression that a hatchet job is in the works.

Remember what Anne says. Establish trust. Get your subject talking. Then you may employ the journalistic equivalent of the Columbo routine—when he gets to the suspect's door he turns around, puts his finger in the air, and says, "Oh, one more thing . . ." It may appear to be an afterthought, but it is the thing on which the suspect eventually hangs. As a writer, be certain you have substantial information about all peripheral issues before you address the issue that may make the subject defensive, and therefore closemouthed. If the subject gladly addresses the controversy in a candid way, you're that much ahead. If he or she does not, at least you have in your notebook or on your tape recorder the essence of a profile.

Trust with the subject, by the way, is much related to trust with the readers. If readers, for example, get the idea early in the

piece that you have a hatchet job in mind, you will not have
persuaded them to continue—to read toward some mysterious
climax. Generally, it is a good rule to follow that early in the
piece the subject of the profile is given his or her due.

In the matter of controversy, rules vary according to subject.
In the end, however, a writer should never shy from addressing
the controversy. It is almost always addressed by the subject in
a civilized way. Besides, your main goal in a profile is to present
as honest a portrait as you can paint, and you must never allow
your concern about the subject's reaction to cause you to pull
punches in the piece. In any case, it is impossible to predict
with any degree of certainty how a subject will react.

Many years ago, I published an excellent profile of a very
prominent businessman in Miami—prominent financially, polit-
ically, and physically. Here was a man who very visibly threw his
three hundred-plus pounds around. At once he was gruff, like-
able, excessive, overbearing, educated, passionate, dogmatic.
The writer, a very experienced magazine staff writer, knew he
had to detail some of the more eccentric circumstances of the
subject's life. Certainly the subject, a very clever man, could
sense from the nature of the writer's questions that sensitive
areas were going to be dealt with—among them his liaisons
with exiled foreign rulers, the way he demonstrated his wealth
very publicly, and even some mention, certainly, of his generous
anatomy. In fact, at one point in the piece, he asks the writer
that he be allowed to hear the negative things being said about
him, that he be permitted to respond. That was not a problem
for us. Such response, as pointed out, is required in a profile.

Yet the writer anticipated, certainly, some negative reaction on
the subject's part when the piece came out, and so did I. In fact,
the very next morning I received a call from the man, who
charged that the writer was a "goddamned Nazi." He urged me
to meet with him in order to show me the dozens of mistakes
that had been made.

It is not my policy to undermine writers. I am more concerned
with encouraging them to do their best possible work than I am
in mollifying their subjects. On the other hand, I have as an
editor an obligation to consider charges that a writer has been

unfair, even when the charges are couched—as on that day—in a slanderous way.

At lunch, I visited the businessman in his office. We chatted briefly at his ornate, hand-carved walnut desk, and I waited for several minutes as he spoke on several phones and in several languages to business associates around the world. When the last call was complete, we adjourned to the adjoining lunch-room, where his butler had brought in a huge tray of sandwiches. I ate one. How many he ate I do not recall. I was more concerned with the physical evidence of my writer's Nazism. He showed me the article. Nearly half of the six-thousand-word piece was underlined in yellow marker. I wondered if he took issue with that much of it. I have always insisted on accuracy when it comes to verifiable facts. That is, the writer is responsible for any errors, even if they are the result of what someone told him or her. Independent research is required. In such a case as this, and with what I knew about the writer, who was an earnest and accomplished professional, I could not imagine so much incorrect information.

Yet, as it turned out, the subject didn't really object to the references that tied him with deposed Nicaraguan dictator Anastosio Somoza, or with presidential pal Bebe Rebozo, or with the description of lavish parties, Rolls-Royces, or the charter flight to Israel he arranged for the hundreds of guests to his son's bar mitzvah. He didn't object to the mention that he had sued two of his employees for slander, or even that rentals were not going as well as he expected in the high-rise palace he was trying to fill. In fact, there were no errors in the piece, he finally admitted. Except for one.

There was just a single point he wanted to make over sandwiches that day. He turned to the fifth page of the piece to a paragraph not only highlighted in yellow marker but underlined in passionate ballpoint red.

It began: "We set out in his Mercedes 600-5, stopping at a Baskin-Robbins, where we each had four scoops of ice cream. . . ."

Amid a world of political and economic intrigue, it was this assertion that had set him off. "Never in my goddamned life have I ever ordered four scoops of goddamned ice cream!" It was, in those six-thousand words, the only reporting that he challenged.

This was the clearest and gruffest example of the writer's need to uncover and write an honest assessment of the subject, without regard to the subject's expectations. Clearly there had been no way to anticipate, when there was so much more at stake, such a clamor over chocolate and vanilla.

✧ 8 ✧

The Middle Ground

Beginnings, Ends, and What You Write First

Many unsolicited manuscripts ago I learned this: be wary of the writer's first few words. This was no singular discovery. William Zinsser, the eminent teacher and author, long ago observed that in their beginnings, novice writers often try to "commit an act of literature." Annie Dillard, the Pulitzer Prize winner and professor, argues that she never pays much attention to the first page of a student's theme. Like Dillard and Zinsser, I try never to form conclusions from the first page alone; I look deeper for signs of real life.

In their attempts to engage readers immediately and impress them with the intelligence of the piece—as well as the skills of the person who set down those words—beginning writers tend to create the most inappropriate and off-putting prologues. As a result of a week's worth of first pages, I become very well informed as to the particular greenness of the grass, blueness of the sky, brilliance of the spring flowers, brightness of the sunshine, or chill of the wind. And there is this sort of beginning, a variation of which you have probably seen any number of times:

"Fred Smith leans back in his chair, takes a drag on his cigarette, loosens his tie, stares out at the parking lot, shakes his head, and sighs. Here is a man clearly under siege."

More likely it is the writer under siege, wallowing without an idea. It is the writer sitting there, looking out the window,

129

smoking, sighing—and employing the present tense in a desperate attempt to infuse some drama into an undeveloped scenario.

Some writers, seemingly aware of the disadvantages of the doddering start, try the opposite extreme. They plunge right into the matters at hand. But they do so too quickly. Such a piece may begin with a recap of what happened, leaving the very first page packed with indecipherable action.

I received one manuscript recently that, deep within it, offered effective and evocative scenes. But the first two paragraphs tried inordinately hard to entice the reader with a catalog of horrors that had been inflicted upon the main character during her years as an activist in South Africa. Such catalogs, no matter how impressive in length or degree, are unlikely to evoke the response intended; they do not serve to bring the subject of the piece and the reader into the same room, to breathe the same air, to feel the same emotions.

Obviously, the wrong sort of emphasis is often placed on the first paragraphs. While it is true that if the beginning is not interesting, it is safe to assume the middle will never be read, it is also true that in terms of substance the beginning of most pieces is often misleading, and is almost never the information that sticks with the reader. It is a mistake to try to coax some emotional reaction out of the first few words. Those critical words ought to be reserved for inviting the reader, catching the reader's eye. The best beginnings are seductive beginnings: literary foreplay.

A writer who has seen or experienced some very emotional and telling episode should be eager to take the reader to the physical and spiritual place; this is the primary reason a writer writes. What the writer often forgets is how he or she got to that place—the emotional prelude to that scene.

Often after a first draft is submitted, I will ask the writer why certain anticipated information is not in the piece. The writer will sometimes reply something like, "It's right there, on page one of the manuscript." And I will admit to having missed it. This is usually not a sign of inattentive reading but of writing manipulated to seem important and compelling that does not persuade or entice readers to drop emotional guards and to become involved. Good writing is important and compelling in itself—in its style, its subject matter, in the authority with which it is presented, in its natural pacing, and in its frankness. Good writing establishes a trust between writer and reader. For that to occur a writer must begin a piece simply, honestly, clearly, reflective of the writer's true perspective on the subject matter, without providing demonstrations of literary contrivance.

Good beginnings are important, and they should not be rushed; they should not mislead the reader into thinking the piece is something other than what the writer intends.

As a writer you will not always have the good fortune to encounter editors who will look beyond the first page. You must impress from word one. The question is how to do it, and the way is much more natural than most writers suppose.

One of the main lessons I have learned about editing and writing is to retain in some way the writer's initial enthusiasm and natural curiosity about the subject. Many times that initial impression is well grounded and very impressive—the writer will brim with enthusiasm when the idea is first presented—and yet when the finished piece arrives it is largely devoid of that passion. Somehow the writer became intimidated by the subject matter, or in some other way lost course, or has been with the subject so long that its freshness is gone. The piece that is finally turned in is more summary than passion, more conventional than personal, more expected, almost as if it could have been written by anyone, not the person who just a few weeks or months before had expressed a singular vision. Often I will remind the writer of the words used to sell the idea, having kept a copy of the very persuasive query letter, and of the initial vision and passion. Where is that passion now? I might ask. That is, where is the hint to the natural beginning of the piece? Why was the writer interested in the subject in the first place? You as a writer make a persuasive case to yourself about why you have chosen a subject. It's probably a very good case. Why not make the same case to the reader? The reader, then, will be just as intrigued by the coming literary adventure as you were when you first proposed it. Then the two of you, writer and reader, are free to continue that journey to the most critical part of the piece.

ॐ ॐ

What interests me far more than beginnings are middles. The middle is the physical reply to the question, "What does the writer have to say?" If the writer has something interesting, compelling, singular to say, and can say it in an entertaining and authoritative way, the beginning and the end become the least of the problems. We polish those beginnings and ends simply by evaluating the middle, and by returning to the initial reason for the piece.

I use the term *middle* metaphorically. That is, if the piece is a narrative—a classic way to tell a fiction or nonfiction story—the middle is likely the chronology of events that in good writing is augmented and enriched by the writer's point of view. Almost any example of classic fiction will demonstrate this.

Mark Twain's *A Connecticut Yankee in King Arthur's Court* tells of a nineteenth-century factory worker who suffers a blow to the head and goes back in time to King Arthur's court. Clever as the idea is, it would not speak as eloquently to the contemporary reader if the story were not just an opportunity for the author to use an engaging tale to weave within the action observations about major issues. Twain comments on slavery, poverty, and ultimately the human race's impressive capacity to do itself in, as well as minor issues such as the idiocy of newspaper editors and the hopelessness of the life of the umpire, a conclusion drawn after his protagonist foolishly introduces baseball to the knights of the Round Table. Yet even Twain had to start somewhere and end somewhere; that is, he had to frame this rich work. He had to offer a reason to the reader to join him in the fantasy of Camelot. This is the function of the prologue and epilogue featuring the voice of the factory worker, with whom readers of the late nineteenth century could easily identify. Readers who may have needed some enticement to return to sixth-century England found it in the engaging and pained invitations of the narrator. The end of the book, controversial though it may be (I won't spoil it for those who have yet to enjoy this remarkable novel), is very much related to the beginning. Such is almost always the case in good writing.

What I am suggesting is that, in writing, the beginning isn't always the beginning. Don't get hung up so early in the process. Just keep writing. The right beginning will often arrive at the end.

ॐ ॐ

Obviously, the structures of classic literature and modern nonfiction are very closely related. Yet there remains the subtle difference that the nonfiction writer must reveal slightly more than the novelist in, or very near, the beginning; the reader must know early on why the piece is there. Such a presence in a piece is the nut graph, or the "nut section."

Here is how Fred Mann, the editor of the *Philadelphia Inquirer* Sunday magazine, a publication widely recognized for its superb reporting and writing, describes the most common approach to the nut section:

"Often, we'll start out with a scene-setter beginning, one that introduces the protagonist in a colorful situation, something that epitomizes his character or the adventure in which he is involved. Then comes a nut section that explicitly states the premise of the story, outlines the major themes, and sells the story by tempting readers with engaging quotes and tidbits of information, and which works as a preview of coming attractions. This nut section is important; it tells the reader why this piece is new and different. There should be enough fanfare about the story's significance to convince readers it's worth the investment of the next twenty minutes of their lives."

Such a formula is good to know. And yet it still depends on the writer's ability to master the material, to make sense out of the research. We return to a piece that we sampled earlier in order best to illustrate the problem and its solution.

Patricia Weiss invested much time and effort to uncover the particulars in the lives of the Cotters, the family found dead in their elegant house in Hartford's west end. The keys to the success of her piece, no doubt, were the answers to these questions: How reliable was her information about the way the Cotters lived? How much detail could she uncover? How well could she reconstruct the character of their lives? How well could she get the reader into the head of the man who apparently decided that his family's prospects were so grim that he killed his wife, daughter, and son? These answers were much more crucial than a clever beginning or end. This is not to minimize the importance of the first and last impressions of the reader, only to indicate that Pat knew that the true effectiveness of the beginning could not really be gauged until the middle— the point—was developed well, so that the beginning and end could speak directly and insightfully to that point.

One of Pat's first attempts at a beginning, written before the research project was completed, would have undermined the piece.

A year has passed since the chilling tragedy on Woodside Circle, a year since the four lifeless bodies were discovered in the mansion with the shades drawn tight. The dust of emotional demolition has had time to settle. People shattered by the loss of an entire family are finally beginning to heal. Why, many wonder, dredge the horror up again?

"It's yellow journalism," declared one close relative of the victims, declining to speak of the incident. Many of those that did talk openly worried about possible sensationalism.

Certainly the story entails enough violence, high living, and intimations of scandal to fill a season on a prime-time soap. But beyond the grim details lie basic human issues that are even more compelling. How could a family with so much to live for come to such a terrible end? If it could happen in an apparently happy household, couldn't it befall any one of us? Painful as it may be to those left behind, when a self-wrought tragedy strikes a seemingly healthy family, it demands thorough investigation.

Even close friends can't fathom where the trouble began. Some remain consumed with denial. Refusing to believe John P. Cotter Jr. killed his wife, daughter, son, and then himself, they suspect foul play was at work. But the few people privy to the Cotters' private world wonder how everyone missed all the signs. One close relative calls the theory that an outsider did the killing "absurd and so out of touch with what was happening with that family, it's incredible."

Another wonders how so many were fooled by their cheery demeanors and privileged airs. In the material sense, John Cotter Jr. may have been wealthy, "but in terms of human relationships, he was the poorest man I ever met."

This was not an unreasonable beginning. The writing was sound. A point of view was clearly expressed. Pat knew she wanted to explore the gulf between appearances and hard reality. But as a beginning it had clear weaknesses. It was too much—too much recap, too much explanation, too defensive, and yet not close enough to the subject matter. That is, to encourage the reader to begin a very long piece, you generally cannot toss a number of theories and summations at them before they have had a chance to identify with the primary subject. This question is never one of absolutes but of subjectiveness. It was my view that Pat's beginning was not quite right but, at the same time, I was hesitant to have her work on it. I preferred that she develop the middle. There were clear enough hints the middle would be very effective—she had talked about the results of her extensive research—and I was certain that once the lives of the Cotters could be reconstructed, a smoother, sparer, more enticing beginning could be fashioned.

The more she learned, the more she drew from reluctant sources, the more authority she gained to write the piece. The need to defend it was gone. And, as time passed, she sharpened her own point of view. As you can now see, the final beginning was drawn from the middle of the story, not from the fringes of the tragedy:

There's one thing you can say for certain about John P. Cotter Jr. and his family: They were close. People say they had everything—two airplanes, a chauffeured limousine, and the kind of boundless, mutual devotion that made them want to enjoy it all together.

The prosperous Hartford developer didn't just love his children; friends say he adored them. "Inseparable" is the word that comes up when they describe the father and son, who were happiest hunting and fishing together. So attached was his daughter to her family that she left her women's college nearly every weekend, not to pursue a social life, but to go home.

Cotter and his wife, Anne, also appeared to be a well-integrated pair. When John began seeing a psychiatrist in the spring of 1989, Anne sat in on his sessions. But people did not suspect trouble in their paradise. Late last June, they were seen walking down the street in West Hartford Center holding hands.

No wonder everyone was dumbfounded when, within two weeks of that blissful scene, John Cotter took those familial bonds way beyond reason. Even friends can't fathom where the trouble began. Some refuse to believe Cotter killed his wife, daughter, and son, then himself. They suspect foul play.

When it happened last July, no one intimate with the Cotters spoke openly in public. People quoted in the press were mostly acquaintances and curiosity seekers found gawking at the crime scene outside the lavish West End mansion with the shades drawn tight. But now the dust of emotional demolition had time to settle. People privy to the Cotters' private world are ready to talk about the tragedy at Woodside Circle, to try to reconcile the turmoil they saw with the terrible outcome they still can't face.

This is a much more natural, less forced, less complicated beginning. In just a few words, it begins to demystify the Cotters, begins to portray them as people, not as mere subjects of headlines. This is done through the judicious use of such details as Julia's tendency to come home on weekends and the father and son hunting and fishing together—what might be seen as positive traits, or traits common to most families, notorious or not. Such observations allow the reader to identify with the subject. The point of view is just as forceful as in the first beginning but slightly more developed and more subtly presented. The tone is one more reasonably reflective of community attitudes a year later; it is sober and appropriate.

This beginning succeeds also because the writer is clearly in command of both the subject matter and the way to reveal it. She implies that details of the family's perils are to come; the reader has read enough to know that what is coming is likely to be evocative. That is, Pat did not give away her best stuff—the details of a way of life that was obviously out of control—but clearly hinted at it.

Note, too, that Pat retained her illuminating observation, "But now the dust of emotional demolition has had time to settle." In the second version, it comes later and is set up better. Where it is now, after the reader has made a slightly larger investment in the piece, gives it greater effect; it becomes conclusion as well as observation. It is an example of the point made all along in this book that good writing is a story to tell, honest detail, and a writer's point of view.

The point of view introduced at the beginning must be reflected at the end; otherwise the piece will seem contrived and ultimately dishonest to both writer and reader. That is, the beginning works if you as the writer can conclude that it is true in substance and tone to the essence of the overall piece. Note here the other bookend to Pat's piece, the last two paragraphs:

> Susanne Spellacy also thinks about how it might have ended differently. She recalls the last time she saw her uncle, on Father's Day 1989. "I considered pulling him aside and saying, 'What's going on in your life? Nothing's that bad.' To this day, I wonder if it would have made a difference."
>
> Then again she has her doubts. "In a way, I kind of feel it was predestined." She recalls what another relative said at the funeral. Gazing at the four caskets draped

in white, she observed the scene made perfect sense. "They died the way they lived," she said. "Together."

As you can see, beginnings, middles, and ends are not subject to unbreakable rules but are primarily the result of your best expression as a writer. Cleverness should not be your primary goal. Action, though important, is not enough. It is more important that you digest your volumes of material, that you think about it, that you work it out on paper, that you master the material by the time you have settled on the final version.

Now you can see the origin of James Ricci's beginning in the Garry Trudeau profile discussed earlier ("Have a lobster on Perry Morgan? Garry Trudeau said he'd just love to. . . .") and of Madeleine Blais's first sentence in the Edward Zepp piece ("All his life Edward Zepp has wanted nothing so much as to go to the next world with a clear conscience. . . ."). Both writers got their beginnings from the middle. They put the reader right there—at the table, on the train. They did not dally or tell too much. The reader had no choice but to read on.

⳩ ⳩

Although it is not necessarily easy to put these theories into practice, it is indeed possible to master them provided your intention, and attention, is serious. Consider the case of Elaine Kramer. She is an editor by trade, and her writing experience was limited, largely composed of the sort of short news pieces that all aspiring journalists must write in their formative years: accounts of zoning boards, town budget meetings, and police news. Never had she written feature stories or magazine articles, and certainly never anything that required great introspection on her part.

Nor had she ever, until the spring of 1988, faced a personal crisis that compelled her not only to reconsider her own values but to share them with hundreds of thousands of readers. Elaine had been told by her doctor that her pregnancy—her first—was in grave danger, and that a drug called DES taken by her mother to prevent miscarriage now threatened her own fetus. In order to prevent premature labor and the certain death of an undeveloped child, she was ordered to spend the final five months of the pregnancy in bed.

In the piece that she eventually wrote, one that took the reader through an emotional adventure with an unimaginable ending, Elaine recalled that time with unusual candor. This moment in the piece was very close to the physical beginning of the narrative:

> I called my mom in Indiana: I wanted sympathy, and I wanted someone to blame. Should I tell her this is probably because of DES? No. She'd just feel bad. But I want her to feel bad. Here I am stuck in bed because of some stupid drug she took. Tell her. NO. That medicine was the best stuff around in 1957. Everybody took it. Maybe without it, I wouldn't be here. She would have miscarried.
>
> Tell her! No, don't.

Although Elaine's story's "middle," which physically was composed of 90 percent of the piece, took several months to write and rewrite, it was in a sense a natural process. Once Elaine decided she would tell the story in a narrative, a major organizational concern was eliminated. That is, she could go back to the beginning of her pregnancy and use the time in bed to weave back to childhood or consider her relationship with her husband, Joel Shaul. Such a narrative approach gives authors, particularly those unschooled in point-of-view writing, a framework for both story telling and observation. In the formative stages of her narrative, Elaine had enormous help from Bruce DeSilva, the *Hartford Courant*'s writing coach, who encouraged her simply to reveal the story in a straightforward way, as it happened.

This narrative was distinguished by another indispensable characteristic: total honesty. There is simply no other reason for writing than to present the writer's singular truth, even though it presents great risks. In this case, something very personal was shared with strangers, and, even perhaps more unsettling, thoughts were expressed on paper about people close to Elaine, her mother, for example, that had not been expressed in any other way.

Bruce also taught her how to set a scene, to describe the details of a place as she had seen it during an emotional time. Elaine told of the traumatic holiday season, the coming of dangerous contractions and their passing, her fear of allowing her friends to give her a baby shower too early, of receiving permission after several months to become semimobile and to attend a childbirth class, and how, after a time, she became "cocky."

> [I] decided it was "safe" for my friends from work to give me a shower. Joel and I needed baby supplies. I needed company. They put up yellow crepe-paper streamers and a "Baby Shower" banner, and brought lasagna, salad and two desserts. We had wine. I had seconds.

The baby was carried nearly to term and weighed well over six pounds, delivered after six and a half hours of labor. "[Peter] had a lot of black hair, Joel's eyes, an uncle's mouth and an undistinguished nose. . . ."

Elaine related her relief that Peter had seemed so healthy, had scored well on the Apgar test, which measures the apparent health of newborns. But within half an hour the doctor returned with news that the baby was having trouble breathing and was being fed oxygen. Soon Elaine heard an emergency call to the nursery.

> Could it be Peter? Don't be silly. Silly was not an appropriate word.
>
> "Sometimes infants have trouble breathing," the doctors said again, but our pediatrician was growing more concerned. He examined Peter once again at 7:30 P.M., when Peter was four hours old, and came to my room to explain to Joel and me that x-rays showed one lung was partially clogged and the other was trying to compensate. It looked like amniotic fluid congesting the lung. OK, so he has a little breathing problem. If he had been

born months ago he would have been in much worse shape. In comparison, a little breathing problem is nothing.

After a team of doctors examined Peter, a nurse arrived with the news that "Peter is much sicker now." His lungs weren't keeping up with the demand and no one could figure out why. How can this be? The pediatrician had just reassured us. It can't be so serious. Her words were measured. She spoke slowly. "I have to tell you this," she said. "Your baby may very well die." DIE? I screamed inside. The room went black. Someone else's baby, you mean, not Peter. Not PETER.

Elaine described the next few frightful hours: the decision to rush the baby to the university hospital, where specialists might offer some miracle solution; the visit from the nurse, who said to Elaine, "When a baby is so sick, we usually bring them in for the mother to see before we go. Do you want to see him?"; her decision to let him go right away instead; the news that Peter was now in extremely critical condition, and that an available lung machine for newborns had to be found; Elaine's indignation, "How dare the sun shine today?", the news that a place for Peter had been found in Boston; and the news, a few hours later, that Peter had faltered once, was revived, faltered again, and was not revived. "The doctors took out all the tubes. A nurse held him while he died."

Elaine describes holding Peter one last time, and then the funeral. And then the terrible punch line. The doctors determined that Elaine's difficult pregnancy had had nothing whatever to do with Peter's death: he had died of a strep infection caught from Elaine in her womb after her water broke or during birth.

It was only a year later that Elaine was able to set this narrative down. In the course of several rewrites she came to terms with all the key questions of the episode: the medical intimacies, her relationship with her husband, her thoughts about motherhood, and about her own mother, and even dealt with the reactions, and nonreactions, of colleagues at work, which she found baffling and distressing. Clearly she had a very moving "middle" to the piece. But the two things she had not solved were where the piece should begin and where it should end. It is possible, of course, to take *The New Yorker*'s approach; that is, Elaine theoretically could have started with her family history, going back to ancient ancestors and finding telling episodes of birthing. Or she could have begun with the news that she heard from the doctor when she was four and a half months pregnant. But if, as a writer, she was trying to give the reader some idea of the reason for the piece, that beginning would fail; it would seem as if it were merely a piece about a difficult pregnancy. A laudable idea, certainly, but not right on. Not the point at all. What was the point? That's the key question in considering beginnings and ends. The point is what determines whether they work or not.

Because the writing was so soon after these events, it was a difficult question for Elaine, yet one she knew she could work toward; the piece, after all, had been therapy, had been a chance, after all the discussions with her own family, after all the introspection, to see if she could find words that made sense of it, that accommodated her feelings.

The first attempt at a beginning avoided the point altogether. A suggestion had been made that, for drama's sake, the piece should begin in the hospital, as the news is delivered that Peter is in trouble. The reader would be quickly introduced to a life-and-death situation. But Jan Winburn, *Northeast*'s associate editor, argued that the real drama of the piece would be undermined by considerations of a quick beginning. There was no way to imagine the particulars of the ending when Elaine was ordered to spend the rest of her pregnancy in bed; that mystery should be preserved.

So Elaine, Jan, writing coach DeSilva, and I undertook "beginning and end" discussions. I explained that often in essays, or even in profiles or narratives, such deliberations are necessary. That narratives suggest themselves. That they are good ways to set down events, and to weave among those events the values and viewpoint of the writer. But the overall viewpoint, the key questions and values, are sometimes outside the physical body of the narrative. That is, a writer must decide why he or she is telling the story, and then the beginning of the piece, and the end, must be reflective of those reasons. Of course, I should never say "always" in a book about writing. Much serious writing does tell the reader why he or she is reading the piece in very subtle ways; good writing can make those reasons inherent. Still, such a technique puts a tremendous burden on the author and sometimes on the reader. In writing for general audiences it seldom hurts, and almost always is a substantial help for both the writer and reader, if the reason for the piece is clear. Why is it written? Why should it be read? How may a writer do this without giving away the climax?

I did not suggest to Elaine that there was some simple answer to this, or that she write the following: "Please, dear reader, see here what happened to me and my baby." What I asked her to do was search within her, to ask herself why she decided to write this piece. "If you can answer that question," I said, "you'll have your beginning. And you'll also have your end." I explained that beginnings and ends are related and often almost interchangeable, at least in spirit. Often when a piece begins nowhere I try to catch a clue about its reason for being from the ending. At such a time, a new beginning can be fashioned by the writer.

This was an assignment Elaine could not easily undertake; she had obviously written a painful narrative. It was not a relishing prospect to ponder days more on the purpose of the piece. Yet she did so; it was typical of the way she took direction—eagerly—and with complete confidence in her editors.

When she returned, she had her answer: the piece had helped her consider her own accommodation of Peter in her life. And an incident that she could now recall became her beginning:

> The young woman pulled red plastic dishes out of the diaper bag and arranged bites of food on the tray of the high chair. She turned halfway toward me as we made conversation. I was trying to ignore her child, but he was hard to overlook.
>
> "Wasn't the wedding beautiful?" The baby threw some peas.
>
> "Isn't Debbie a perfect bride?" The baby spit up.

"The weather sure held up." He squealed.

We had finished our shrimp cup and were on the main course. The mother and I were running out of pleasantries. The baby was making more noise than the three-piece jazz combo. I decided to try to converse with her as I might have a year earlier. "Your baby looks like he's about six months old," I said.

"Spoken like someone who knows," she replied. "Do you have children?"

Her question caught me off guard. I had expected her to talk about her own son.

"How should I answer?" I thought.

I twisted the white dinner napkin in my lap.

"Don't say it. Don't bring it up. It will just make her uncomfortable," I thought. "But you have to answer. Say something."

This was Elaine's prologue. From there she picked up at the point when she was four and a half months pregnant, where she began her carefully woven and candid narrative. Such a beginning promised two endings: news of what had happened to the baby and a more spiritual conclusion—what perspective does Elaine now give to the life and death of her child?

Here is the end of her piece:

I sat in meetings (at the newspaper) where we discussed stories about infants found frozen to death, babies thrown in dumpsters. I went to the bathroom and cried.

Everywhere I went, I saw babies. I never knew there were so many in the world. I hated teenage girls with children. Once, in a grocery store line, I chewed out a young mother who slapped her child for being cranky.

Joel and I had three weddings to attend during the summer and we hoped they would lift our spirits. Over Memorial Day weekend, we went to my friend's wedding in Chicago. Next to me at the reception was the young woman with the baby. He was few months older than Peter would have been.

The baby hadn't been invited, and my friend, the bride, apologized over and over that we were at the table with him. The other people there were my cousins and dear friends. They know what to talk about and what not to. But on my left was this woman with a baby. How could I be so rude as to not speak to her all evening? How could she be so rude as to bring an uninvited baby to a fancy wedding reception?

I stuck with safe subjects until I ran out. When I said her son looked about six months old, she had responded with the question for me.

How should I answer?

People don't mean any harm when they ask that question. For them it's like discussing the weather. But for me, to say I have no children is to say that Peter wasn't real. It is to deny how precious he was, to deny how much I wanted him and how much I miss him.

Don't say it. Don't bring it up. It will just make her uncomfortable. But you have to answer. Say something. "No, I don't have any children. I don't have any children, but I wish I did."

Thus Elaine Kramer finished her first serious piece of writing. The piece touched many readers; they wrote letters about their own losses. Some writers in the community were inspired to compose similarly private essays. And the following spring, the Sunday Magazine Editors Association chose "A Baby Called Peter" as one of the three best essays of the year—not for its beginning, not for its ending, but for a middle that no one who read it will ever forget.

℘ 9 ℘

Funny Business

The Art of the Humor Writer

Every magazine wants to offer readers a good laugh, but few deliver with regularity. This is because humor writing is perhaps the toughest writing of all, and therefore, in an odd way, may offer the best opportunity. You needn't worry that there is an overabundance of hilarity in the publishing world. But how do you know if what you write is funny? Even if you get your wife or husband to laugh her or his head off, does it mean a prospective editor will?

At a meeting of fellow Sunday magazine editors in 1982, I quoted from the work of a largely unknown writer, a man who had been forced to make his living organizing writing seminars for businesses. Reading aloud, I laughed so hard I nearly choked on the words. At a particularly hilarious moment in the narrative, I looked around the room at my fellow chokers. Only they weren't choking. Two others were chuckling, four smiled, six appeared on the brink of becoming amused, four frowned, and one shook his head, as if to say there were more serious matters (and there are, of course) to consider in this all too serious vocation and all too serious life.

I don't want to sound as if I alone appreciated the early Dave Barry; other editors used his early work. (In particular, Gene Weingarten, as editor of *Tropic*, was Barry's biggest champion, convincing *Herald* management to hire a writer who could easily have been dismissed as "juvenile" by terminally serious editors.) But I do think it is worth noting that even someone whose books now regularly make the bestseller list and who is commonly regarded as perhaps the funniest writer in America does not make everyone laugh. Humor, just as all other creative writing, is a subjective matter. Or as Dave Barry, in his particularly erudite manner, would observe, "Boogers."

Truth is, as much as I think of Dave Barry's writing, I would not classify it as "humor," at least not in the traditional sense. Dave is a writer of comedy. He is more of a joke teller, and a superb one. His hyperbole is based on real-life situations and taken to a joyous extreme that only his inventive mind can imagine. To suggest that anyone can be Dave Barry would be ludicrous. Ample evidence arrives weekly from ersatz Dave Barrys, just as in the past Erma Bombeck seemed to be lurking behind every suburban front door. Cheap imitations will never do.

On the other hand, humor can be a wide-open door. Anyone who can laugh can write some form of humor, or at least the hint of humor. Humor is wry, elegant prose infused with observation, irony, and juxtaposition. Did you ever read, for example, Roger Angell's study of the art of the baseball catcher? In an early spring training game, the batter hit a foul ball into the dirt. The ball bounced up into an area in the rookie catcher's anatomy that is generally not pinpointed in the press. The catcher was bent over, his knees resting on the ground, his head staring straight into the earth as he "waited for that part of the day to be over."

It is dangerous, even foolish, to dissect humor. But it is obvious enough that "waited for that part of the day to be over" is a gentle, lovely way to describe a pain in the groin, which if revealed more graphically and less artfully would become a mere joke, and a crude one at that.

It is pretty safe to say that, as much as you may admire Angell or James Thurber or Mark Twain, you should take only the lessons away, not the specific style. What they produced is natural to them—entirely their own expressions. As I believe that every writer has a unique voice, I think that every humor writer sees irony in a special way.

I do not advise, for example, that all prospective humorists should set out to write "hilarious" pieces, only pieces that reflect their natural voices. Nor do I necessarily think of humor as a special category set aside to be used only with very light subjects. Humor is almost always useful to break the tension of a piece.

It is true that any writer's manual will tell you basics about humor. There is the saw that misfortune is funny. True. But misfortune alone doesn't do it. Perspective, juxtaposition, pacing, the setting up of the funny lines are what is required in humor. In the end, much depends upon the belief that humor matters, that it can make a difference.

James Thurber once wrote, "Every time is a time for humor. I write humor the way a surgeon operates; because it is a livelihood, because I have a great urge to do it, because many interesting challenges are set up, and because I have the hope it may do some good."

Jay Maeder, a Sunday magazine editor of considerable note, apologized for the delay in calling me back. "The staff and I were sitting here all morning reading aloud from Colin McEnroe's new book. We were laughing our heads off. We couldn't get any work done."

This was the second volume of McEnroe humor to hit it big. The first, *Swimming Chickens & Other Half-Breasted Accounts of the Animal World*, had been a collection of columns. This one, *Lose Weight Through Great Sex with Celebrities! (the Elvis Way)*, was a little more expansive, and drew more on Colin's singular view of life.

His introduction explains some of this:

> I'm sorry about the title.
> We went right down to the wire on a choice between this one and *Anna Karenina, Part II*, but in the long run, nobody felt up to hashing things out with the Tolstoi family lawyers. . . .
> Well, you can't second-guess yourself forever. When

people ask me why I wrote this book, I tell them it's because I believe it's time that somebody stood up and spoke the truth, because they don't teach values in the schools anymore and because I needed, in order to satisfy certain obligations incurred at my local jai alai fronton, the kind of pecuniary assistance that only a large, unfeeling American corporation such as Wedtech or Doubleday could provide.

Note the juxtaposition in the last paragraph of high moral purpose with a reference to his own gambling debts—a fraudulent reference, as the reader can tell, but the sort of juxtaposition that is at the heart of humor. The use of Wedtech, a scandal-ridden corporation, in connection with his own publishing house is risky. Risk is a valuable tool of the humorist.

Colin has not written enough pieces for me to suit my taste, but he has written enough topical and biting humor to be syndicated in hundreds of newspapers. One day I asked him to talk about the craft of humor writing, as if he were counseling those who might want to emulate him.

The first thing I found is that if you want to emulate Colin McEnroe, you first have to be convinced early in life that your humor doesn't matter, and is secondary to "real" writing.

"I can remember trying to write funny stuff in the third grade. The assignment was a serious one—to write a serious paper. The teacher had not mentioned the word *funny*. But I decided to write as if Huckleberry Hound, the cartoon character, were talking. The teacher was mystified, said it wasn't funny, and handed it back with a quizzical look on her face. She said I used phrases like *on account of* and that I had to do the assignment over again. This has been my life. Do it over again. Don't be so funny."

Many years later, after graduating from Yale and landing a job at the *Hartford Courant*, Colin was obliged, not surprisingly, to cover the news—a somewhat humorless task. "The only funny things I wrote were little comments I'd put up on the bulletin board. Other reporters were the only ones who read them." But for Colin, humor was a compulsion, wide audience or not. "One day, humor writing may pay for itself. If you wind up doing it for a living, chances are you've had this weird compulsion all your life.

"A person doesn't really get much encouragement nowadays to become a humorist. Jobs don't appear under 'H' in the classifieds. You just have to keep going at it.

"It's not only that people are accustomed to getting their yucks watching television. In the sixties and seventies humor writing went out of fashion. All there was was the lowest common denominator, like Andy Rooney, or the incredibly rarified and cerebral, like Veronica Geng. The middle ground disappeared. Now, it's coming back with Dave Barry, Garrison Keillor, Roy Blount. Blount advises that humor is once again timely because it does well during 'times of ill-advised cheerfulness.' The Reagan era needed lots of cynicism. Bad economic times help, too. I think we are entering another era where humor will be welcome."

Even if you want to take advantage of this timely opportunity, you must understand the hole from which you must climb. Colin thinks his experience in school was not unique, that whatever natural humor a person has is extracted by the time it is necessary to make a living.

"High school is when you are at your funniest. College is the great ruinating unmaking of a writer. How often there—or afterward—do you get rewarded for writing something funny? To be funny, you have to say to hell with the consequences."

Probably more than any other kind of popular writing, humor writing is the loneliest. "It will help you to figure out what works and what doesn't. While you write something, and someone says it is not funny, there are two possibilities—the person just doesn't get it, or it isn't funny. One of your jobs is to trust your instincts."

Another job, Colin says, is to be scared. "A humorist is like Wade Boggs, from day to day. He doesn't know if he'll get a hit, or if he'll go three for three at the plate. It's an elusive thing. The harder you try the worse you make it. One of the tricks is to loosen up. Don't think about the process. It's like thinking during sex, 'Am I having a pleasurable experience?' instead of just having it. I have my best results (writing) if I know what I'm trying to say, or when I'm trying to alter the rules. Free association works. Juxtaposition. The more, the better. Like in fiction, you have to think about extremes. Think about the best things and worst things that can happen to your character. So if you're writing about installing an air conditioner, you have to have ideas about real extremes, and then pull back, but not too much, and it makes sense. And, of course, use nose hairs and boogers and insult the Elks Club wherever possible."

♫ ♫

The best thing about humor, Colin says, is that if you make people laugh, you can say anything, even insult their political opinions—an area notorious for sobriety.

Here is a column written right after the 1988 vice-presidential debates. It is the one column out of thousands, Colin says, that he would not change a word of. He was happy with the pacing, the words, the story telling, the edge, and the commentary. It is safe to say, however, that Dan Quayle appreciated none of these. The piece focused on the moment in the debate when Quayle was asked by Tom Brokaw to reveal any philosophies from his formative years that may have shaped his politics. After attempting to evade the question, he could only come up with a quote from his grandmother, who told him that if he tried hard enough he could do anything he wanted. Colin wrote a brilliant satire on the lack of depth and thought in this campaign in the style of a country humorist.

> Years have passed, but I can still remember it, plain as a pea on a pile of potash.
>
> Papa was looking out the window at the neighbor's boy, little Danny Quayle, just standing out in his own back yard staring off into space the way he always did.
>
> Papa drew back from the window and mumbled to no one in particular. "Land sakes, that boy doesn't have a whole lot of buckwheat in his pancake, does he?"
>
> "Sshhhhh," Mama said. "They'll hear you. The Quayles have high hopes for that little Danny."

"They can hope all they want. I always said you can't pluck peacock feathers off a drawn duck."

"I always said," Grammaw chimed in as she toted laundry up the back stairs, "a one-legged cricket can't kick a pickle barrel through a half-ton of jackstraw."

"I always said," said Uncle Gaylord, climbing down the attic stairs, "you can hook a catfish with a —"

"QUIET!" yelled Mama. "Don't you know those poor Quayles don't have any sayings? How do you think they feel hearing all your colorful sayings floating out the windows night and day? How do you think that poor little Danny feels knowing he's going to grow up with no anecdotes to shape his philosophy? I always say you can't grow corn in a —"

"MAMA!" we all yelled.

"Oh, my," said Mama.

Those poor Quayles. They really were anecdote-impaired. They were saying-deprived. They had a lot of echoes in the cracker barrel. One Christmas I remember seeing Mama sneak out the back door with a basket covered by a checkered cloth.

"What you got there?" I asked.

"Ohhhhh, I just made up a basket of expressions and adages and a couple of parables and homilies for the Quayles," she sighed. "It's Christmas, and we have so much, and they have so little."

We used to hear them sitting around the dining room table trying to develop a homespun philosophy.

"You can't throw . . . something down . . . some kind of hole and expect . . . something," Mr. Quayle would say.

"Carrots," Uncle Jeb Quayle would say.

"You can't throw carrots down . . ." Gramps Quayle would try.

"Aren't carrots already down a hole?" Mrs. Quayle would ask.

"You can't take a cat out of . . . a chair if, ah . . ." said Cousin Norbert Quayle.

"If a dog is . . ." said Mr. Quayle.

"Carrots," said Uncle Jeb.

We just felt so bad for Danny on Wednesday night when that mean Mr. Brokaw asked him for a story or a saying from his life that shaped his philosophy. We all thought, oh, Mr. Brokaw, if you only knew the kind of childhood that boy had.

I remember one time I was over at the Quayles' and somebody had put one of those framed needlepoint samplers on the wall. It read, "Home is good."

"Gee," I said. "Don't they usually say, 'Home, Sweet Home' or something?"

"Home what?" said Mrs. Quayle.

"That's terrific," said Mildred Quayle Quackenbush. "Did you make that up?"

"Get a pencil and write that down, Mildred," Mr. Quayle said.

"I sure will, quicker than . . . something very fast," she answered. "Home Sweet . . . how did that go again?"

"It there a comma in there someplace?"

"Carrots," said Uncle Jeb.

It took me half an hour to get it all worked out for them.

"I feel sorry for little Danny," I said when I got home to my family.

"That boy is a few logs shy of a cord," Papa said.

"He's kinda all bell and no clapper, ain't he," Uncle Gaylord added.

"I don't reckon he got quite enough mercury in his thermometer," said Grammaw.

"Shhhhh," Maw said.

And then, in the stillness, we heard little Danny's grandmother singing him to sleep with that song she always liked.

Be a fairly good person.
It's better than being a worse 'un.
Always look where you are going,
Especially if it was recently snowing.
And don't drink coffee when you walk downstairs,
Because da da da something something.

> And just as the lights went out, we heard someone say,
> "Carrots."

One of the elements of Colin's humor in this piece was certainly the repetition of the word "Carrots." It is a funny word,
obviously, but, more than that, humor generally depends on
such repetition, the reintroducing of absurdity at critical points
along the narrative.

Colin quotes Roy Blount's observations that a piece "should
be funnier than necessary." Get to the joke, and then top the
joke. Don't make it a one-joke or one-premise piece. Though
dependent on the premise of a word-poor family, the Quayle
column required continual invention—stranger and stranger
phrases as the piece went on.

Colin explains further with a visual example. "The delight in
the cartoons of William Hamilton [whose work appears in *The
New Yorker*] is that these cartoons—so elegantly and richly
detailed—are funny because Hamilton has gone to such serious
trouble over such flimsy concepts."

As you note from the Quayle column, Colin is a practitioner of
story telling. "People are most comfortable reading stories—it
pulls them along, it allows them to come in and out of the dark.

"In a story-telling motif, you can weave almost anything into
it. You can stop a story to mention Newt Gingrich, for example,
no matter what the subject. Try to jumble a lot of things. If you
are writing about snow tires you can bring in Ibsen or Schopen-
hauer. If people don't get the joke, it's OK. They don't have to
get everything."

Colin suggests that it takes a lot of writing to perfect humor.
"Of a hundred columns I did years ago, three or four were
worth preserving, and still would be fresh. Now twenty-five to
thirty of a hundred are worth keeping around. My ability to
discern has made the difference."

Like most good writers, his inspirations require instant attention. "If I get a nice little idea and come back to it five or six
days later, it turns out terrible. I've got to write it right away or
it gets stale. Spontaneity in humor is important. If you get the
spark, run for the keyboard or it's gone forever."

For that spark, Colin reads and listens. He pays attention to the news, to conversations, even to radio talk shows. "You learn much from the way people speak. They'll flat out say stuff that's worth copying down."

He regularly reads the work of novices. "Some of it is pretty funny, but needs polish. As it goes on it starts to run out of energy. When you write, you must relax, not try too hard. Once you get going, don't let them see you sweat. Just like stand-up comedy—you have a natural flow."

As for selling humor, he says, "If you're reliable, on time, you'll never go hungry." Colin is regularly in demand by national magazines to bring levity to their otherwise heavy editorial agendas.

On the other hand, if it scares you, you are not alone. "There is not a more doubting, ridiculous branch of writing than humor writing," Colin says. "I don't think there is one writer who wakes up and says, 'I think I'll write some great humor today.'"

And remember this, a philosophy of life that his un-Quayle-like mother issued long ago. "When I was in the fourth grade she said if I don't change my ways I'll become a derelict and urinate on cars. Nowadays I have a dream in which a green Pontiac becomes the object of my mother's worst fears."

ஜ 10 ௺

At Your Service

Innovative Approaches to Specialty and Consumer Writing

At his *Northeast* farewell lunch in 1984, Bryan Miller speculated about what might happen to him at the *New York Times*.

He had written restaurant reviews and food columns for me for many years, and he had done a superb job. I had perpetually observed that the *Times* would need someone to replace Craig Claiborne and that eventually Bryan would be a prime candidate. He knew his subject, and he was a fine writer and a person of obvious integrity. Yet when the *Times* finally called and offered him a job as a food reporter, he said that he hoped that it would not evolve into restaurant criticism.

I suspect the hesitation had less to do with fear of the big time than with Bryan's natural modesty. Food criticism is high profile, and the business of restaurants, "foodies," and celebrity chefs is bizarre and backbiting. Bryan had always been comfortable with a modest profile and steady professional progress.

He had started slowly, very slowly; it had taken a long time to build up his confidence. When he wrote his first review in 1976 for a small daily newspaper, he could barely place his order; he was obliged to consult a French dictionary to identify the dishes. At that point, he had two realizations: he had a great interest in the subject, and he had few qualifications to write about it.

So he made a very large investment in himself. He became a waiter and cook at Restaurant DuVillage, an establishment of wide reputation in Chester, Connecticut. In an elegant dining room and, as he described it, a "panicky" kitchen, he learned the subject of food from owners Charles vanOver and Priscilla Martel in a way that he could never learn from books or simply by dining out.

After he acquired such inside information, he became a very successful, if continually uncomfortable, critic. Writing sets you up for the judgment of others, judgments sometimes hard to swallow. When you make your living as Bryan does, assessing the work of others, you set yourself up for especially harsh assessment of your own work. This inevitability came clear in his very first review for me when he gave a less than glowing account of his experiences at a hotel's new dining room—the very same hotel that had taken out an eight-page advertisement in the magazine on that very Sunday. The review began with a general and not very flattering observation about the nature of hotel dining rooms and proceeded into specifics as to why the Parkview Hilton's fit the sad stereotype. It was capped off with this observation about the dessert:

> The cheesecake, however, merits special attention, for it was a marvel of modern food engineering. It looked like cheesecake, with its gooey blueberry sauce on top. But it was totally devoid of any hint of dairy products. It had a rubbery, gelatinous texture and all the flavor of ice cubes. I'm sure its shelf life was marked in seasons.

I shielded him from the manager's angry phone calls, but he eventually learned of the fallout. He knew that there was a reaction, too, when he gave a lukewarm review to a restaurant run by the most distinguished restaurant family in Hartford. After giving the Carbones their due for decades of culinary dedication and excellence, he nevertheless took exception to the pâté at their new restaurant. Bryan had pointed out that it tasted frozen. Carl Carbone called me the next day, dismay in his voice. "Can you have lunch?" I did so, at which Carl asked me to sample the food of which Bryan had been critical. "Now, does that pâté taste frozen?" Carl asked. "No," I said. "But I'm not the critic. If Bryan says it tastes like it's frozen, then he has a perfect right to indicate so in the review." Months later, Carbone confided that Bryan's assessment was not especially harsh. "It's just that we had been an institution in town so long. And it's the first time the press had ever kicked us in the ass."

Not that Bryan's job was always to address that part of the anatomy. The main duty of reviewing, he knew, was to divine the inspired cooking from the ordinary—it was to recommend, not to ridicule. And yet even in glowing assessments there were dangers.

Bryan wrote a favorable review in which he said the only thing wrong with the newly opened Gloria's French Cafe in Madison, Connecticut, was Gloria herself. Gloria Pépin, wife of famous chef Jacques Pépin, argued she wasn't even there when Miller came to assess the food. Recently she said, "The reason I'm not in the restaurant business now had a lot to do with Bryan Miller. I'm pretty thin-skinned. I just couldn't take his kind of stupidity." When she unexpectedly met Bryan at a dinner party, and the host suggested he crash at his home for the night rather than make the drive back to New York City, Gloria chimed in with a suggestion of her own: "Why don't you crash on I-95?"

Well, you can see just a small hint of the difficulties in doing this kind of writing. Like Bryan, you can become qualified through training and inspiration to get the job you want. You must earn the editor's trust so that the editor will stand up for you. You must exercise your best, most honest judgment. And you must be able to take the heat.

Because writing is such a subjective matter, and criticism is always called into question, I can only suppose these were the sources of Bryan's hesitations about New York. I didn't see Bryan again until five years later, in the summer of 1989, when he invited me along on a research trip for a *Diner's Journal* report. I met him at a posh hotel on West Fifty-Seventh Street. He looked happy and, as usual, you would not suspect from his waistline that food is his living (a more precise description here would not be appropriate; I have promised, as all his friends have done, not to describe his appearance in order to maintain his anonymity in restaurants.) As we sampled salmon in puff pastry and other representations of haughty cuisine, he said he had warmed to his position as the profession's most prominent critic and had learned to take the criticism in stride, even Frank Sinatra's. Bryan had written that Patsy's, one of Sinatra's favorite places, was "mundane and overpriced." The entertainer was moved to purchase an ad in the *Times* that attacked Bryan's judgment.

Bryan merely brushed it off. He knew such attacks came with the territory. He still enjoyed writing about food—the writing itself was the reward, not the public reaction.

Actually, Bryan's experience as *Northeast* food critic had been rather tame compared to that of his successors, Jane and Michael Stern—also self-taught foodies, who met in graduate school at Yale. Their style was far more aggressive and emotional than Bryan's and drew, as you can imagine, more emotional responses from the public. Even though they left *Northeast* years ago for *The New Yorker* and to write more books, including the very successful *Encyclopedia of Bad Taste*, there are still readers who go around quoting some of the Sterns' best lines about culinary bad taste, including ones penned about one of the most historic Connecticut restaurants.

They described the sauce for the broccoli and cauliflower as a "repulsive pool of yellow liquid." The honey butter was like "an old refrigerator . . . closed with the power off for a few days . . . a yellow, oleaginous paste wax, decoratively swirled into a small white ramekin." About this restaurant, they felt "like Ralph Nader must have felt when he figured out there was something extremely wrong with the Corvair."

The Sterns saw themselves partly as culinary Naders, defenders of public taste, blowing whistles on overpriced, underachieving restaurants. They felt that any establishment that charges substantially must be held to the highest standards, and that the bruised feelings of the owners are not to be considered as consequential as those of unsuspecting customers who drop $150 for paste wax and accompaniments.

Such no-holds-barred assessments drew letters from readers that crossed the lines of decency, many of which I printed and which, I suspect, were as hurtful to the Sterns as their reviews were to some restaurateurs. Yet I felt obliged to print them; the Sterns were in the business of opinion, and they were fair game.

The Sterns will always be remembered by readers for their candor. I will remember them for their enthusiasm. They could be as ebullient about an honest diner as the fanciest of the French.

About Timothy's, an unpretentious lunch spot that features homemade specialties, they wrote the following enticement:

> It feels like a privilege to eat at Timothy's. Although it is a nonchalant neighborhood lunchroom with paper napkins and rickety wooden chairs, no one who loves honest good food could fail to be inspired by the rarity of the dining experience available beneath the Sprite sign for $5 or less every day across from Trinity College.

And later in the review is this example of the most effective of restaurant reviewing, a description that jumps right off the page:

> The sign on the wall says "North Carolina pork," but Timothy's pigmeat sandwich is more luscious and appealing than most of the vinegary barbecue platters you will get in the Tarheel state. The pork is chunked and shredded, bound in a devil-may-care hot sauce, heaped into a thick hunk of whole-grain bread. The other half of the sandwich is mounded equally high with cool homemade coleslaw—a perfect balm for the heat of the "Q." The platter is a sandwich only in name: it is far too messy to be eaten with anything other than a knife and fork.

In their farewell column, they summed up restaurant reviewing in this wry way:

> What truly interests us about food is not so much the way that linguine tastes. It is the personality of the restaurant in which the linguine is served, the avenue . . . on which the restaurant is located, the way in which the

linguine expresses neighborhood and regional character. As critics, we deal with those matters of local color,
but only as background to what readers rightfully demand to know: "How's the linguine?"

જી ભ્જ

Food writing is, of course, just one example of the opportunities
in specialization. In the last couple of decades, the media has
increasingly focused on the categorization of life. Such a trend
has created a tremendous market for specialized writing. If you
had an interest, say, in writing only about walking shoes, you
could make a fairly reasonable living crafting pieces for *Walking*
magazine and as a special walking shoe correspondent for all
publications interested in seducing people who regularly put
one foot in front of the other.

This phenomenon is no secret. Thousands of writers already
focus their energy on specialties. So you may think, "Is there
room for me?" Such a question, though natural enough, has only
one answer: "Yes." You could search through all these fields,
talk to all the highly successful writers, and you would not find
one who did not feel, in his or her formative years, the way you
may feel today—that there is no chance you can crack the big
time. How did they do it? In most cases, just like Bryan Miller,
by cracking the small time. The key to any specialty writing is
that initial investment.

A word of caution: one of the prices of success in this field is
the very good possibility that you will be pigeonholed, that
when you are ready to write your novel or your definitive biography of Winston Churchill you will be fielding endless calls
from periodicals or book publishers or even talk-show produc-
ers who need your expertise on matters that have been explained a thousand times. This is because success breeds success: once you have been published, you will be noticed by
other publications. You will be amazed at the demand for your
writing. So it is critical—just from a time point of view—that the
subject in which you specialize is one that makes a difference to
you. Do you enjoy writing about food? About gardening? About
science? Such questions are as important—more important—

than any perception of the marketplace. The market will accommodate one more food writer, one more medical writer, one more expert on automobile repair, provided that such a writer brings something new and passionate to the field. There is no point in faking it—editors and readers will know.

One of the advantages to focusing on a specialty is the marketplace itself. Magazines, for example, are by and large marketed products. With the decline of the general interest field, publishers seek defined demographics. There is pressure for service pieces, for the opportunity to reinforce the reason that readers are buying one particular magazine over another. The other side of that, of course, is that there is less and less room for literature, as short stories or nonfiction narrative are not necessarily quantifiable in terms of audience. I am not saying that you should not write the latter, only understand why it is that ordinary service writing may be easier to sell than an inspired short story. If, for example, you researched the subject of carrots—do they really help your eyes?—you could sell such a piece to any number of newspaper science sections simply for the idea, no matter what the answer to your question actually was. But if you wrote the modern-day equivalent of, say, "The Celebrated Jumping Frog of Calaveras County," the mails would seldom bring cause to jump for joy, but would supply observations such as, "According to recent focus groups and readership studies, not too many of our subscribers have interest in reading about frogs who are weighed down with lead. Couldn't you write, instead, on ten wholesome ways to get your frog to jump farther?"

꙳ ꙳

The emergence of Nancy Pappas in the field of medical writing is a sterling example of the need to follow instincts and interests.

Reflecting on a career that took many unexpected turns, Nancy says, "You don't ever get a certificate saying you're such-and-such kind of a writer. It simply emerges.

"All through my schooling, I felt a big tension between science and writing. I never had science anxiety, even as a young girl. In fact, I almost changed to a chemistry major halfway through college, but decided to stick with history. There was always a little side theme to my life of liking science. And yet I was surrounded by literary people who didn't like it, and who didn't understand it. So I began to think it was not worthwhile."

Nancy went to graduate school at Columbia, studying journalism for the first time, and then qualified for a reporter's job at the *Hartford Courant*. "I did political writing, where you had to deal, of course, with politicians. And it was horrible. I was more interested in the medical reporter's beat. He did interesting stories and got to read the *New England Journal of Medicine* every week."

Eventually, as tends to happen in the news business, good reporters become editors, and Nancy began to supervise the medical writer and other specialists. When the medical writing job came open, she took a "demotion."

"I liked the idea of taking things that were technical and intimidating but important, and making them accessible without compromising accuracy. A million people were chasing after the governor to get a quote but almost nobody was doing this sort of work. I also found I liked dealing with scientists, doctors, and researchers. They're smart, they like what they're doing, and they like to talk about it, especially when they know you'll get it right.

"People often ask me, 'Oh, what kind of training do you have,' and I say zip except for a college biology course. But when you write about a subject for a long time, you get it right. The interest level has to be high—that goes for anything you do—or you'll be bored and won't do a very good job."

Nancy's on-the-job training is in stark contrast to her husband's work as a music critic. Steve Metcalf, a gifted and elegant writer, came from the inside of the profession with a classical music education and years in academia.

Where Steve never had to question his authority with the subject matter, Nancy did. Therefore it took time for her to gain the belief that she could make it as a science writer outside the confines of an institution—that she could become a successful freelancer.

Yet she was not happy with the way the newspaper covered medicine at the time; it did not seem to respond to a subject of increasing importance and interest.

An incident occurred that convinced her it was time for a change. A local competing paper had reported chaos at an elementary school. "The kids were rehearsing for a program, and one kid got sick and threw up, and then suddenly a couple of dozen kids were fainting and not breathing, and all were rushed to a hospital. There was total panic. Two hours later, they were all discharged, and all were fine. The paper said there was suspicion of toxic fumes. I looked at this situation, and, although I was not an expert on mass hysteria, I figured it might have been just such a case. The state health department had been called in, and I knew a guy in that office. He agreed it was mass hysteria, which he said was a fairly common thing. I went to the medical library and looked up cases, and they matched this perfectly. One kid was legitimately sick, another girl saw her being carried out and got sick, and then the parents said, 'My kids aren't crazy. There must be toxic fumes there.'

"I went to my editor and said I wanted to write about this. He asked how much time I needed. I said a few days to talk to teachers, kids, parents, emergency room personnel, and the like. The next day, he said he would take the story but I couldn't go down there for the interviews—it would take too long. 'Do it over the phone,' he said. So I did. I never set foot in the school. I wrote the story and they liked it well enough to put it on page one, but it was not the story it would have been had I been able to go there and describe the children and the school. It made me realize that the news management was not really interested in anything good, only in what I could do for them on Thursday for Friday's paper. They were willing to compromise a story. And this was the compromised story that gave me the push I needed. I didn't need that torture. Besides, I had two little kids at home, and hoped that I could work there."

Nancy wanted to take the risk and see if she could drum up some freelance work. And from day one she had more than she could handle, including two projects for *Northeast* that turned into compelling pieces. The first was about a poisoned house;

the insulation had infected the air and made the owners perpetually ill. The second piece, the winner of the New England Newspaper Association award for feature writing, was called "The Triumph of Beth Usher," a narrative about an eight-year-old girl who required a rare operation in which half of her brain had to be removed. Nancy spent a great deal of time (nearly a year) on the piece, and was sent by the magazine to Johns Hopkins to be present for the operation.

Meantime, work piled in. "I usually had many pieces lined up in advance. Within a year, I was to the point of having to turn things down on a regular basis."

Some of the work that was time-consuming was for national magazines. Her first assignment was the result of query letters. "Sometimes I got photocopied rejection letters and sometimes more personal notes such as 'We can't use this, but how about something different?' and sometimes it was 'Sure, we'll take it.' Once I wrote one thing for a magazine, the people there would usually call back. This happened at *Woman's Day, Medical World News*, and other magazines.

"And when I appeared somewhere, people called me up from out of nowhere. I got a call last winter from *Parenting* magazine, asking if I wanted to write something, and then called back and asked if I could write something else. And *American Health* called and asked if I would write for them, and then later wanted to know if I was interested in an editing job." (She wasn't.)

Freelancing was going so well she would take no full-time editing position—but writing might be another matter. One day she was looking through the *New York Times* want ads and found that *Consumer Reports* needed a medical and environmental writer, someone who enjoyed taking complexities and making them enjoyable. Someone with editing experience. "They were asking for me." The trouble was, the office was well across the Connecticut line in New York State. Her husband, Steve, said, "Too bad it's so far away. Maybe they would let you do the work from home." Nancy says, "Such an idea was crazy." But it worked. They hired her and let her stay home.

As last words, Nancy offers a couple of pieces of advice. She says that in consumer writing you learn more and more about the subject but you have to constantly remind yourself that, writing for a general audience, you must be sure you ask and answer the basic questions. Your readers, after all, know much less than you do about the subject.

The other point pertains not only to consumer and specialty writers but to all who write. "Basically, you can't be embarrassed about your work or qualifications," she says. "You can't have any false modesty."

ふ ん

For a young woman who didn't seem to have a chance at landing the job she sought, Debbie Geigis seemed remarkably poised and confident. She was aware that her competitors for the position of *Northeast* consumer editor were far more experienced. And she also knew this: she had great belief in herself. Debbie was ebullient, imaginative, and unabashed; within the confines of a thirty-minute interview she must have offered a dozen story ideas.

Her résumé was illuminating, but needed some amplification, particularly the reference to the "Glamour Don't." She was eager to explain. For many years, *Glamour* magazine carried a regular feature that pointed out to readers ill-advised fashion and grooming. The technique was to take candid photographs of people on the sidewalks. When it became apparent that such a practice might eventually be challenged in court—that the right of a magazine to ridicule unsuspecting souls might be a qualified one—the staff looked for one of its own to be singled out for humiliation. Not that Debbie's appearance suggested this move, but as the youngest in the office—and the writer with the biggest feet—she was well qualified to demonstrate that month's point: ugly foot fashion. She was such a sport, and she did her modeling with such enthusiasm, that she became a Don't for All Seasons. That is, until the season she unexpectedly showed up at our office door.

Even as a Don't, she clearly learned a lot of Dos, most significantly the Do that is at the center of good consumer writing: the sell. You must sell the idea, you must sell the point, you must sell yourself. A few days after the interview—in a week we allotted ourselves to mulling over our selection—she offered more evidence of her abilities than we had sought. It was the gutsiest and most imaginative pitch for a position I had ever witnessed. The mails brought a mock-up cover of *Northeast* on which her profile appeared nine times, with her eyes blacked out in the fashion of the old Glamour Don't, and with the cover lines, "A Glamour Don't Admits: I *do* edit."

We couldn't help but be caught up by her positive attitude. She had made us so enthusiastic about the magazine we knew she also had the keys to reader interest: timely ideas, energy, and great care. We had no choice but to hire her, and it is safe to say that, although I have suffered no shortage of talented staff members, no staffer in twenty years has had such immediate impact. Consumerism, which had generally been a competent but uninspired part of our content, suddenly became a strong point. On weeks when cooking or fashion or travel or home entertaining had dominated the magazine we had often been sent into fits of discouragement, even boredom. Now these were rivaling some of our best issues.

In addition to developing consumer issues, Debbie conceived and organized an innovative column for *Northeast* entitled "The Wise Guide," which not only keeps readers up on new con-sumer developments, but also tests and challenges new writers. She makes liberal use of many who, like her, are not long on experience but who are willing to jump in without reservation.

The first thing Debbie tells them about consumer writing is not to call it consumer writing. "I think it's such a dreary term. It conjures pictures of coupon-carrying shoppers in crowded grocery stores contemplating boxes of neon-colored detergent. This genre of writing doesn't have to be dull.

"Sure, you have to have all the nuts and bolts info—time, dates, cost, addresses. You have to do the legwork for the reader, and that legwork involves fine, detailed points. The reader doesn't have the time to plan the great weekend vacation, so the writer becomes the travel planner. The reader can't be bothered to watch for a hot, reasonably priced wedding present, so the writer becomes the personal shopper. The reader doesn't know what it means when her car goes URG! TCKKKKKK! PST! so the writer becomes the mechanic.

"Good consumer pieces pass the readers fictional quarters—

something is in their pockets that wasn't there before: good information."

Information, of course, can be a killer of prose, boilerplate and boring, as in, "Here are six reasonably convenient laundromats." But Debbie says, "Done right, consumer writing is bright, fun, and helpful." She issues her guidelines in three basic categories.

௯ ௷

The Hot Idea. "For a summer travel series, we challenged our writers to come up with better local haunts than the familiar ones listed in chamber of commerce manuals. That took some digging. The state of Connecticut is small, and sometimes it seems like every stone has already been turned. Not so. Many reporters, through driving in their cars or hitting the library or simply asking around, uncloaked excellent destinations. One writer, assigned to cover the Litchfield area, wasn't satisfied with recommending a museum, church, or the proverbial town green. She made lots of phone calls and uncovered a gallery featuring drawings by famous artists for *The New Yorker* that didn't advertise, and would only be open for the summer. She clued the reader in to a local secret.

"You must search for these secrets. Some days, you won't have to search very hard. One writer, relaxing with the classifieds of an underground paper, found a tiny ad for a new delivery service for condoms. The resulting story in *Northeast* was picked up by the Associated Press and run nationwide. Another writer walked through her hometown and discovered a small flyer taped to a florist shop: 'Save a greyhound.' She called the number and found a woman who rescued retired greyhounds from cruel deaths. The resulting article placed dozens of dogs in caring homes."

௯ ௷

Write with Energy. "Use quotes, descriptions, puns (and know when not to—when the subject is a sober one). Also, it's always worth making the trip to the location, instead of being satisfied with a phone interview. It will give you specifics and inspiration."

The beginning of a story about a fifties restaurant:

"Pull those saddle shoes, poodle skirts, and letter sweaters out of mothball storage, slick back that 'do (a little dab'll do ya) and bop on down to Hartford's Pratt Street for a taste of Craig & Company, a '50s-style diner with a decidedly '90s flair."

From a piece about singles night at the laundromat:

"One recent Friday, a small group of mostly thirtysomethings ready to wash their dirty linen in public gathered in the Hamden store, clutching detergent, hangers, and lots of quarters. Dee Dee organized volley balloon. Then Bill ('What's an iron?') won the scavenger hunt with Beverly, who later shimmied her way to limbo victory with Henry, an Arm & Hammer detergent man."

ʃʰ ɾʲ

The Twist. "Rather than hit a subject head on, try to think of a novel approach, something that hasn't been written about.

"A writer couldn't get inspiration for a travel piece by exploring the area by car. So she took a hot-air balloon ride, saw the region from a new angle, and wrote a fine story. Rather than reporting on the opening of a new museum room after it was formally dedicated, a writer visited the "work in progress." Her "piece" listed those involved in renovations (two designers, four painters, six upholsterers, etc.), which added up to an astounding number. She enticed people to the event by revealing the efforts behind the scenes.

"Instead of simply reporting that Oliver Peoples' sunglasses, at $178, were the rage, the writer found a pair of knock-offs for $50, photographed the two side by side, and asked the readers to tell the difference. A reporter discovered a new-age store just opened in her neighborhood. Rather than writing a dry piece about the opening, she created a glossary of crystals and their effects.

"None of the above pieces spared the details, but they did reveal those details with style."

And they all subscribed to the method at the heart of any effective writing: going there. And, like Debbie, going all out.

🔊 11 🔈

Market Wise

For the Shy Writer, the Art of the Aggressive Sale

The spring of 1980 was a season of extremes in the Blais/ Katzenbach household.

Madeleine Blais enjoyed a series of success stories—good fortune that became abundantly clear to an audience of elderly women when the emcee listed three recent events in the luncheon speaker's life. "Maddy has just won a Pulitzer Prize for feature writing." There was polite applause. "She has just bought a house in Miami Beach." The applause was louder. "Finally, ladies—she has just gotten married." The audience cheered.

Marriage may be the best news of all to senior civilians, but to writers it may understandably share billing with the act of writing, being published, and collecting rewards for that work. And, at that moment, only half of the household had all her acts together. Maddy's husband, John Katzenbach, was getting unfavorable and dispiriting reviews.

John and Maddy's new house was in mid-Beach, right around the corner from mine, and I would often stop over for a drink after work, a ritual that necessarily included updates on the great experiment in John's professional life: his first novel. To write it, he had given up his job as a reporter for the *Miami News*. "Sitting there, covering the criminal courts, I knew I wanted to be a novelist. So I was really sitting there with my eyes and ears sharp, and trying to accumulate information to put in a book."

Having made that commitment, John's livelihood and self-esteem rode on his success at writing and selling.

John's agent sent the novel to thirteen houses, one by one. Each took its good old time. Each invariably offered the same maddening final judgment: no. "The most infuriating," John recalled, "was the [rejection] from Little, Brown. The novel was taken to the editorial board, and it failed by one vote. They wrote, 'We wish success to the house that publishes it,' but there was no such house, and I was screaming. Then the guy from Simon & Schuster said the book starts too slowly. Another said it starts fast but ended too slowly."

I remember thinking during that time—and expressing such thoughts to John—some common wisdom about writing: stick in there, don't give up, keep your chin up, etc. I worried that John would see those expressions for what they sounded like, and yet I actually believed them—provided the writer doesn't stop at homily worship but actually does the sticking, actually doesn't give up, and keeps that chin in a lofty position.

For one thing, I knew John had talent. Yes, I know I have argued that everyone has talent. But John had enormous natural gifts that had already been sharpened by years at solid reporting. "One of the luxuries of being a journalist," he told me, "is you hear things profoundly crazier than anything you can make up as a novelist." What was profoundly crazy in this instance was that John had a good story to tell, he was a good storyteller, and yet he got no positive results.

I do not set myself up as the ultimate judge of a writer's worth, but seldom are such instincts far off base. My instincts come to the fore when I work closely with a writer.

While he was waiting for those publishing houses, he wrote for me a perfectly crafted, hilarious tale about a make-believe major league baseball team in Miami that wins the pennant largely through the use of voodoo. His characterization, dialogue, and narrative were masterful. This clearly was the work of superb writer. How could he be rejected so as a novelist? He couldn't be. Not in the long run. Someone out there would see, would sense, his gifts. And that eventual publisher's taste was proven when John's book, *In the Heat of the Summer*, became a bestseller and was then made into a very successful movie, *The Mean Season*.

I bring this all up because no serious writing book can afford not to dwell on the dreariest of subjects: rejection. As writers, we all take this phenomenon personally, as if we alone have been singled out for such horrors. We take it as verification that we have no talent, that we're wasting our time and the time of the editors who examine our work, that we ought to get work making something that has a physical presence so that at the end of the day we can say, "There, I've nailed a good heel on that shoe." How do our sentences rate? Our magazine pieces? Our novels? Our poems? Our plays? Who is really to say?

First, you need to know you are in very good company if you do not receive universal acceptance of your work, and—I can guarantee this—you will not. Even when a piece is accepted, there will be those on the staff of the magazine or publishing house who will not share your champion's enthusiasm, and there will be carping critics once you are published, many of them people who think they could do better and would have if only they had the vision and energy and follow-through that you demonstrated.

The list of the oft-rejected and unfavorably reviewed is long and impressive. Going through some ancient copies of *The New Yorker*, I came across the magazine's only reference to Steinbeck's masterpiece, *The Grapes of Wrath*, during the season it was published. It was in one of those little quotes and commentaries at the bottom of a column of type, the spot where ridicule reigns. The magazine quoted how many times (ten) the author had employed the word "hams" to indicate a part of the body. The impression left was that this was a work clearly unsuited to the sort of praise it was receiving elsewhere.

At least Steinbeck's work had been published with some dispatch. Other masters required more patience. Latch onto a copy of the recently published compendium of horror tales, *Rotten Rejections: A Literary Companion*, edited by Andre Bernard, and you will see the excellent company you are in or will no doubt join. You will take comfort in the particular insults to the work of, among others, Pearl S. Buck, Sir Arthur Conan Doyle, Herman Melville, Henry James, George Bernard Shaw, Walt Whitman, Oscar Wilde, and even Anne Frank, whose diary brought this response from one house: "The girl doesn't, it seems to me, have a special perception or feeling which would lift that book above the 'curiosity' level."

Writing is a very personal challenge, and it takes time, patience, and grit to succeed. It also takes useful selling tools, for you must not leave your success to fate. And the more you know about how publications and publishing houses choose material, the greater the chances you will find a market in a timely fashion. Such success feeds on itself and bolsters writing confidence.

Soon after I wrote these words, the phone rang. It was a writer whose name and work had been unfamiliar to me. And, as it turned out, my own work as an editor was unfamiliar to her. She was about to compose a query letter and wanted to know if I bought freelance pieces, and how long those freelance pieces usually ran, and what sort of pieces they generally were, and what was the nature of my magazine, etc. I answered all of her questions politely, but privately thought that she was wasting her time. She didn't know enough about the magazine's contents, even after grilling the editor, to write a competent query. It would have done her a great deal of good to have been a regular reader, or to have requested, as most successful freelancers do, sample copies.

It is wise to know everything you can about the publication when you get an editor on the telephone. We editors are, I am forced to admit by the voluminous personal evidence, vain. We like to know that writers have been paying attention to the content of our magazines. Yet, even more important, the more a writer knows about the magazine, the easier it is to sell a particular idea, because an argument may be made by the writer as to how it fits into the magazine's general thrust and personality.

For example, you may point out that the magazine has been in the forefront on social issues but has not yet done a piece on child abuse. You may tap into an area that the editor knows has been a weak spot and wants to address.

Also, knowledge of a magazine inevitably convinces the editor that the writer's judgment is worthy of some attention, for it is on such intangible evidence that decisions to invest in a writer are sometimes made. Editors are very impressed, for example, by a writer's energy and interest level, by the homework already done. If you know what is in our magazines, if you put your proposals forward with a clear sense of purpose and with exuberance, we pay attention.

From your perspective—perhaps walled off from the inner sanctums of the publishing industry—you should take heart in knowing that editors need you, that they can't survive without you. But you must make the best case possible. Remember this: we have chosen to do this kind of work because we enjoy selecting writing that is inspiring and illuminating. That is, such work excites us both as editors and as readers—and we delight in the prospect of sharing it with thousands of others. We are trying to present, after all, magazines that contain that most necessary of all ingredients: must reads. Inevitable stories. The can't-put-it-down piece.

Fred Mann, editor of the *Philadelphia Inquirer* Sunday magazine, says he subjects freelance pieces to the "Turf Builder" test. "Our magazine is the home of creative writing in the midst of this massive Sunday paper. Because we are such an optional read for people on Sundays, we'd better have something that's very good, and different, or they won't read us. That's why we employ for prospective pieces the 'Turf Builder' test. Is this piece something readers are going to devote a half an hour to on Sunday or are they going to go out and spread their Scott's Turf Builder?"

Issues of successful magazines are not unlike productions of hit plays or musicals: they must entice, and they must be presented with enthusiasm, wit, depth, a sense of style, and boundless energy. That energy begins with the writer. If you do your background check on our magazines and you believe in what you propose, even acknowledging and allowing for the natural nervousness induced by the process of presenting so subjective a product as writing, you will likely gain the ear, and eventually the heart and mind, of the editor.

John Dorschner, a superb writer for *Tropic*, not only believed in the story he was peddling but knew the characteristics of his editor. He appeared at my door, pointed his right index finger at the ceiling, and pronounced, "Bury My Heart at the 7-Eleven," to which I replied, "Sold!" He had given me, with ebullience, only the title to his proposed piece, but from that title I could tell exactly what he had in mind: an article about how Native Americans in contemporary society have succumbed to, and have been damaged by, white culture. His title was obviously drawn from an already developed point of view. If John had said, "I would like to take a look at the status of Indians in America," he might indeed have been offering the same piece. But he wouldn't have sounded excited. I wouldn't have been excited. What prospect would we have had of exciting our readers?

There is of course the danger that a writer might sell too hard. When a writer in Miami inquired about the status of her piece, I gingerly told her the reasons why the article could not compete well for space in a magazine that offered a home to only three or four major features each week. That utterance turned out to be the last sample of civility in the exchange, because she responded with this assessment of her work: "It is certainly better than that garbage you printed last Sunday."

She may have been right. But editors—wise and judicious as they may be at selected times—are unlikely in the future to call upon a person who employs this particular argument on behalf of her work. It is much better to point out the redeeming value that you see in your work and why such work would enhance the magazine.

However, one of your arguments shouldn't be the classic "I've shown it to a lot of friends, and they all think it's wonderful." This is an approach used often, and I am often tempted to suggest in reply, "If those friends are so fond of it, why not let them publish it?"

Of course, offensiveness is not an uncommon commodity in

this business. I remember an educated, bright young woman who made her living as a belly dancer and who sent a piece that, not surprisingly, touched on matters of anatomy—but not only hers. She offered documentation of the relationship she had had with comedian Jackie Mason, including a fairly detailed assessment of his capabilities at lovemaking.

Despite the taste concerns, I had a fondness for the article: it was gossipy and lively. And it revealed Mason in the midst of a professional crisis. This was many years before he went on to star in a very successful one-man Broadway show, when he was telling the same old jokes at the Aztec Motel in Sunny Isles, Florida, about as far from the Great White Way as he could be. He was largely a forgotten man, the result of a slide that had begun the night Ed Sullivan thought the comedian had gestured obscenely on the air.

Yet, although the belly dancer's piece was a revealing picture of a man who had once been a king of comedy, something was wrong about its tone. With their relationship apparently over, it seemed as if she wanted to use my magazine to gain some revenge. It was classic kiss-and-tell, an approach that I admit had some great temptations. But when I finally told her of my reservations, that it seemed gratuitously unkind, she didn't ask what she could do to improve it in order to make it suitable. She didn't want to know if references to Mason's anatomy were objectionable. Instead, she turned her attention to my own body; rather than accept my reasoned arguments, she blamed the rejection on my own apparent lack of the particular body parts that she had admired so in Mason. And other insults far too graphic and tasteless to document here followed.

It goes without saying, but I am happy to say so anyway, that such a demonstration tends to turn an editor into an unsympathetic soul. And it also undermines the integrity of the piece; suddenly the editor will question, with some justification, whether the writer was telling the truth about the subject.

It turned out that the comedian himself was somewhat better at the art of the sale. He called the next day. "So, I hoid you're not using the piece." "That's right," I said. He argued, "I thought it was pretty funny. Didn't you think so?" He had a point. I told him that part of my objections had to do with the unfair portrait of him. "So what? It's only woids." It was understandable that at such a point in his life any publicity, even such graphically personal publicity, would be welcome.

I never published it. And, as a footnote to the story, I learned a decade later that we hadn't hoid the end of it. The belly dancer sued Mason for, and won, support for the two-year-old daughter who was the product of their "ended" relationship.

ঌ ৎ

It should be obvious by now that selling is an inherent part of the craft of writing, and sometimes just as tricky. Yet you are not selling snake oil. You are selling honest and worthwhile work. There is a reason you undertake writing: somewhere deep inside you feel that it will be worth reading. You must prove that in your writing, and present your writing forcefully—but not offensively—to the marketplace.

ঌ ৎ

Techniques of selling, much like techniques of writing, can be learned. Even the shy writer—for there really is no other kind— can master them. For evidence, I offer the career of Steve Kemper, a writer who makes a fine living at freelance work.

My first recollections of Steve are from the early 1980s, when his pieces appeared in a weekly alternative newspaper in Hartford. He had proposed to my new magazine a piece on Clemens Place, an old apartment complex near Mark Twain's Hartford house that had been rehabilitated in the hope of drawing more professionals to the city. Steve's work in the weekly paper was respectable, but I wasn't certain if he had yet established the reporting depth to investigate a project that had started promisingly but developed serious problems.

Put yourself, if you can, in Steve's shoes. He had made modest money writing reviews and anything else the weekly wanted him to write. "My policy when I began—and I think this is a good one to follow for any beginning writer—was, when you're first starting, always say yes, and always be on time. I never missed a deadline and I always said yes when anybody called, no matter how hard the assignment was, no matter how unappealing, no matter how little pay was offered for the work that had to be done. And even when the work—as it was in most cases—was on speculation. As a result a lot of editors called me at the last minute. I didn't hem and haw and leave them in the lurch. Editors value that incredibly."

I know that I valued Steve's willingness to investigate Clemens Place even though the combination of research and writing would be so demanding that he would, in effect, be making barely more than minimum wage. He seemed to intuit that his time and effort could never be properly compensated for with this project but that it might lead to something more lucrative. He was willing, just like all writers who eventually succeed, to make an investment in himself.

"That piece involved so much in the way of tracking people down: disgruntled tenants, tenants-rights activists, and state and federal officials. It was a real paper trail. A lot of facts and narrative to keep moving forward and control. I felt for the very first time I was a reporter as well as a writer."

When it finally came in, I knew it had shortcomings. Yet it revealed a writer's promise. Steve offered an affecting description of the human condition, a mature perspective, and a pleasant if unpolished style.

At this point I began to think of Steve as a substantial resource for my new magazine even if I didn't really think of him as a polished writer. When something had to be done, there was a willing, eager hand to do it. He was happy to learn, to put in the hours, and he always got results. Such a writer is indispensable to any editor.

I began to use Steve's work more and more. Then something critical happened, which was a turning point in his life. At various times he had come into the office when I was short-handed for editing help. He would pitch in and spend hours in front of the word processor addressing the work of others. Soon both a full-time and a part-time position came available, and in both cases I asked Steve to apply for the jobs. No, he said. He wouldn't apply, nor would he be available for any more fill-in editing work, no matter what the pay. He had decided to devote himself full time to writing—to making a living as a freelancer. Despite the temptation of a regular paycheck, writing was what he wanted to do, and he was dedicated to pursuing that course.

He could make only a modest portion of what he needed for living expenses from *Northeast*. He clearly had to diversify. "I answered want ads. [He looked under the categories Writer, Editorial, and Freelance.] I did business writing, ghost writing, newsletters on data processing and banking, and other pretty boring things. Anything to keep going. I wrote texts and short stories for textbooks for grade school. I did reviews for public radio for a year, even though I got no pay—it made me feel good about myself and my work. It made me feel as if I was becoming a writer."

Steve recalls that time with particular sensitivity to the fragility of the would-be writer. "In order to market yourself, I found, you first have to market yourself to yourself. You have to believe you are a writer and that you can do what you hope to do, which is get an assignment for money. The only way to do that is to have the nerve to tell yourself, 'Yes, I am a writer. Nobody may know it yet, but I am going to act like one.' You just have to have the guts. You must just do it."

And so he did.

And as he did, he learned more and more not only about writing but about the tricks of marketing.

If, for example, he hasn't worked for a particular magazine before, he does not approach its editor. He goes to an assistant editor. "They will take an interest in you much more quickly, because they read the mail. When I sent an idea to the *Boston Globe* magazine's assistant editor, she said no to the particular idea, but also that she really liked my clips and that she would like to work with me. You have to plunge right in there when you get such an opening. And eventually I did a piece for them."

Over the years, Steve applied two basic rules: "Just ask," and Garson Kanin's observation that "Amateurs hope, professionals work."

"I think what stymies a lot of inexperienced writers is that they're afraid they're going to waste somebody's time or get blasted, or it's really hopeless, so why try? These are all things to keep you from taking the first step—they defeat you before you get out of the starting block. You have to understand that 90 percent of the time at the beginning the answer will be no, but at least it will be something other than your own voice asking, 'Why bother?' It sounds hokey but it's all true. When I was just beginning, and I was getting all the rejection slips, at least I could curse the editors' benightedness, their lack of vision and discrimination about me as a writer. At least I could blame someone else, not me. And as for Kanin's comment, I say this. It doesn't do any good to want to be a writer. You have to pick up the phone. You have to go to the library. You have to do the grunt work."

Steve argues—and it is an argument backed up by his own record—that there is no such thing for a writer as an insignificant job. He took pride in everything that had his name attached. "Even those pieces that I was getting paid peanuts for I spent a lot of time on. Because they were not just pieces for that day, but forever. It sounds sappy but you always want to do the best job you can. Nobody's going to believe your excuse, 'I did this fast but I could always do a better job on it.'"

Eventually, Steve got more and more assignments and could weed out the jobs that seemed less appealing to him. He turned out excellent pieces for *Northeast*, including "Four Against the World," which won a prestigious writing award; it focused on four inner-city teenage girls who competed in the international double dutch competition. On its surface it may have appeared to be only a piece about games, but because of Steve's rich perspective and reporting it was a brilliant commentary on the dreams of city children.

Eventually I recruited him to do a weekly interview column that has become a financial foundation for him. And Steve has been able to market many of those pieces through the network of Sunday magazines.

As his momentum was building, he learned more and more tricks of the trade. "When magazines call about reprint rights, for example, they immediately become a market for you because you know they like your work. Also, any contact is a good contact, no matter how tenuous."

Steve's relationship with *Smithsonian* magazine is a good example of pressing forward, using every opportunity. "First I sent a query to them, and got a decent response. They said they already had a story in the works about the subject I proposed. Then the next month they ran a story on a subject that I was getting ready to send them a query about. I used that as an excuse to call. I said, 'Look, I'm right on the money with what you want. I'd like to come down and talk to you because I'm right on target.' " That was a beginning for Steve, and the open door to a market he coveted.

Now, years after he made the decision to become a full-time writer, other temptations still abound. One company offered him $60,000 a year to teach its executives how to write, and sweetened the deal with the promise of a quick $20,000 raise. But Steve resisted. He would not have had time to write. And writing is the point.

Now, a full decade since that Clemens Place piece, Steve has developed style and confidence. Not long ago he proposed a series based on his personal life. He wanted to document at regular intervals his and his wife, Jude's, first year of parenting. "No," I said. "You'll just be reinventing the wheel. Childhood, after all, is not a new thing." Steve, as I knew he would, pressed forward. "Let me give you the first installment. Then judge." "Well, all right," I said, having nothing to lose.

Need I tell you that "Parenthood: The First Year" became one of the most popular and beautifully crafted series in *Northeast's* history? It was funny, serious, telling, and truthful. And it was a demonstration, too, of the art of the persistent writer. The very art that you—shy you—can certainly master.

🙤 12 🙦

Isaac Bashevis Singer
and the "Hole Story"

Lessons of a Writer in Perpetual Motion

Writers learn mainly by writing. But they also learn by reading, by appreciating the genius in others, by deciphering how a natural storyteller appears to deliver a tale so effortlessly. And sometimes, rare times, writers learn unforgettable lessons in the actual company of masters.

One of my early role models was Isaac Bashevis Singer, whose stories are rich in magicians, fools, and demons and yet rooted in real life; his characters transcend the streets of Warsaw and Manhattan's Lower East Side. They speak nonsense as they speak universal truths.

In October 1978 his work received universal recognition. The *Miami Herald* revealed that Singer, a winter resident of south Florida, would be awarded the Nobel Prize for Literature.

Such happy news was more than recognition of the writer himself. His devoted readers were also complimented for their taste, and I was only too pleased to share the acknowledgment. Yet there were other considerations at work that balmy Miami morning. I wanted to meet Singer. And I had an excuse to do so.

As editor of *Tropic*, the thought occurred that I might convince Singer to write a story that would appear the very Sunday, December 10, that he would receive his Nobel medal and check for $165,000. In doing so, I could present a sample of his work to the more than one million readers of *Tropic*, most of whom knew this author, if they knew him at all, in name only. These readers then could more eagerly and honestly join in that day's international appreciation.

There was, however, little time; the magazine's copy deadline was four weeks prior to its publication date. The story would have to be produced almost overnight.

I looked under "Singer" in the telephone book and found "Isaac Bashevis." A man answered the phone.

"Hello."

"Hello. Mr Singer?"

"Yes," he replied. "This is Mr. Big Shot." (Big Shot is a common phrase in his stories, never used in a complimentary sense.)

I identified myself, congratulated him in a fumbling sort of way, and asked him if he would consider writing for the magazine.

"Yes," he said, "but I have no time. I have to be in Sweden on December 10. Perhaps, my friend, you could use a story I have already written."

Although that solution wasn't my first choice, I said, "That would be fine."

"Why don't you send someone over to my place and we'll pick something out."

As an editor who also writes, not taking the opportunity myself was unthinkable.

"Would it be all right if I came out?" I asked.

He said, incredulously, "You, the editor, would come to my house?"

On the way I stopped at a florist, wondering, What do you get a person who has just won a Nobel Prize? and settled on an uninspired bouquet of carnations and roses. I found Singer's building without much trouble. Although it was a pleasant enough condominium, and had the advantage of the Atlantic Ocean at its backyard, the ordinary white facade and blue-green trim did not suggest residents who commanded worldwide attention.

Alma Singer, the writer's wife, answered my knock. "Good morning," she said, smiling. Mrs. Singer accepted the bouquet, directed me to the living room, and explained, "Isaac will be

out in a moment. He is on the telephone with old friends." She
asked if I would please sit down and have a butter cookie and
some tea, which I did. "Thank you." I said, noting the many
other floral tributes that had arrived that morning. Not knowing
what else to say, I offered the obvious: "You and Mr. Singer must
be very happy about this news." Mrs. Singer, an angular woman
with a strong, determined face, resumed her position at the
kitchen table, where she was writing letters, and waved her right
hand with nonchalance. She said, "Well, Isaac has won many
awards before. That book award last year, what was it?"

As I waited, I read upside-down cables on the coffee table:
"Congratulations" . . . "You deserved it" . . . "At last" . . . "Mazel
tov." And I examined what seemed, its sensational ocean view
notwithstanding, to be an apartment that might have belonged
to a retired actuary: pale blue carpeting, white curtains, and
traditional furniture. There was no sign that a world-class writer
lived on the premises save one: in the corner of the living room,
on a table—not a desk—was the very typewriter, I surmised,
that Singer used to write his stories. I left my seat for a closer
look. The typewriter was manual and very small, and it had
fewer keys than the standard model: the Yiddish alphabet has
only twenty-two letters. All of Singer's work is written in that
rich language, and then translated, sometimes by the author
himself. It seemed odd—and inspiring—that *Gimpel the Fool*
and *The Spinoza of Market Street* and *Enemies, a Love Story*
could have been created out of such a small machine that would
seem to have limited possibilities. Twenty-two keys. Infinite
combinations.

שׂה רעה

The master of those keys emerged from the bedroom. "Hello,
my friend," he said, extending his hand and bowing a little. "My
friend," I came to realize, was a phrase he used easily, a label
extended even to literary critics.

Singer seemed shorter (five feet, seven inches) than I had
imagined him, and thinner (146 pounds). But, at seventy-four,
he was not frail. His expression and his keen blue eyes showed
energy and interest. His movements were lively. On this day

when he may have been excused from formal dress, he had characteristic writing clothes on: a thin brown tie and a white shirt the back of which had escaped the brown pants. He explained that he had not gotten much writing done—it troubled him when a day went by without working at his craft—but that he was enjoying the attention all the same.

As we sat on the couch I repeated the idea I had expressed on the telephone, and he repeated that he could not write something new. Perhaps I would be interested in a story he had just written but not yet sent to his agent for sale. The story, he said, was "an experiment." The idea of having a new piece by Singer after all was thrilling, but when I began reading, my enthusiasm ebbed. It was a story about a boy in outer space—certainly far both in physical distance and in spirit from his customary style. He was writing something about which he knew little, and it was obvious. Singer, too, must have known of its shortcomings, because he didn't press the piece on me. He said, "I don't think it's right for you. Or perhaps for me." And, by doing so, he saved embarrassment all around—and made a sad commentary on the writing life, of rejection even on the very day of receiving a Nobel Prize.

We wondered what to do next. Then Alma Singer turned from her letter writing and said to her husband, "What about the story you wrote about Miami Beach, 'The Hotel,' I think it was called? It's a beautiful story."

"Ah," her husband replied, and then he frowned. "I don't know where it is." He did remember that it had once been published in *Hadassah* magazine, and that it was about a retired New Yorker in Miami Beach whose doctor and wife would not allow him to do anything that pleased him, a circumstance that inspired him one sunny day to rebel. It sounded perfect, but Singer said he didn't have a copy of that issue and wasn't sure if he could locate the manuscript. He disappeared into the bedroom and emerged a few minutes later with what should have been good news.

Although he had found the manuscript at the bottom of his bookcase, it was not really the entire story. He explained that the original piece was very old and that somehow it had gotten damaged. Now in the middle of each page there was a hole perhaps two inches in diameter. Dozens of words were missing. He was clearly disappointed. He sat on the couch and pulled the first page very close to his face, hunching over it. He tried to reconstruct the sentences. He read aloud, "Here on Lincoln Road . . ." He stopped. "I think maybe it says, 'almost like New York.' No. It was so long ago that I wrote this, I can't remember what's missing." What a shame, I thought.

Then Alma Singer said, "It's all right. The gaps are very small. You can fill in the words." I could? Her husband nodded.

I barely knew what to say. A man who had taken such pain to get words right during his lifetime was entrusting an incomplete manuscript to a stranger. I insisted that my own solutions to the missing parts would be a last resort, that I would try to find the edition of *Hadassah* in which "The Hotel" was originally printed.

As it turned out, I never had to do my own impersonation of Isaac Bashevis Singer. I located the printed version of the story and restored the missing parts. The treatment in our magazine obviously pleased him, and he asked if we couldn't go to lunch sometime. "Fine," I said. "Would tomorrow qualify as sometime?"

The lobby of the condominium in Surfside now showed evidence of a resident's achievements. The bulletin board announced a special dinner in Singer's honor. In front of the elevator was a temporary display that contained a black-and-white photograph of the writer dressed in white tie and tails, bowing before the King of Sweden, and underneath the words, "Do You Want Chicken or Fish?"

It might have made a nice irony in one of his stories, of course. And, over a vegetarian lunch that day, we smiled about it. We also talked of his satisfaction in writing for *The New Yorker* ("The editing is perfect. In that magazine, my stories never had a spelling or grammatical error"), how he gets his ideas ("Every encounter with a human being gives me inspiration for a story"), why he still wrote books for children ("Children don't read critics"), what Hollywood did to *The Magician of Lublin* ("It was awful"), and why he is a vegetarian ("Animals shouldn't suffer because of me"). What we didn't talk about, because I would steer the conversation from it, was my own writing. Although my column appeared each week in the magazine I edited, it was not a body of work that was likely to have enjoyed scrutiny by Nobel Prize winners; it represented my own struggle for a voice. My currency was subjects that were intimate, events that occurred in the day-to-day of making a living or in living a suburban life. It was an attempt to develop both a unique style and a worthwhile point of view about the very unusual community in which I lived.

Singer had his own observations of south Florida, his own intimate view of the population, drawn largely from neighbors. And he could say a great deal in a very few words. Here, for example, is a paragraph from *Old Love* about what it is like to live in a retirement condominium in south Florida. Singer captures truths in his fiction that have eluded the *Miami Herald*'s decades of publishing facts about south Florida's elderly residents:

> A week doesn't go by that someone doesn't give up the ghost. They're all rich. The men have accumulated fortunes, turned worlds upside down, maybe swindled to get there. Now they don't know what to do with their money. They're all on diets. There is no one to dress for. Outside of the financial page in the newspaper, they read nothing. As soon as they finish their breakfast, they start playing cards. Can you play cards forever? They have to, or die from boredom. When they get tired of playing, they start slandering one another. Bitter feuds are waged. Today they elect a president, the next day they try to impeach him. If he decides to move a chair in the lobby, a revolution breaks out. There is one touch of consolation for them—the mail. An hour before the postman is due, the lobby is crowded. They stand with their keys in hand, waiting as if for the Messiah. . . .

And yet this is only Singer warming up. Because when his stories get specific—characters developed in detail—they become unforgettable. Gimpel the Fool is, in the reader's mind, forever defecating into his bread dough; Israel Danzinger of "The Hotel" is madly shifting a forbidden cigar in his mouth once the juices of big business start flowing again; and Shosha, the little heroine in the novel that bears her name, remains vulnerable and yet somehow triumphant. Singer talked of the necessity of individuality of character. "Fingerprints must be made so that we can recognize one character from another. When a person doesn't have his own speech he is a cliché. A human being has a face and every human being has a face like no other face. Literature is not about types but about characters. Be specific. The more specific it is, the more believable. Get to the core of the character."

During that lesson, a joke occurred to him:

"Two men meet on the street. The first man says, 'Goldberg, since you came to America, you used to be a tall man. Now, you are a short man. You used to have a red beard. Now, you have a black beard.'

"The second man says, 'My name is not Goldberg.'

" 'Oh? In America, you even changed your name?' "

Singer talked about the craft of writing as not so much a calling but a mistress and compulsion. And his story, for any writer, is illuminating and inspiring. For half a century it had been the same: rising early, having breakfast, working until lunch (usually bread and some cheese—"What choice does a vegetarian have?"), two hours of walking in the afternoon during which he planned his writing. "I plan what to write. How to write. The writer must plan a lot, and, in spite of the planning, he doesn't write according to the plan. While you write a novel, the action keeps changing all the time and it has to change all the time because human life is full of surprises and so is literature. If it is real literature, it is full of surprises. In other words, things happen not according to plan—in literature as in life. Just the same, it is good to have a plan."

He was the consummate example of learning by writing—

having labored for decades before it was possible to make a living at it. Alma had to work at a department store in New York most of her married life. She said, "When you marry a Yiddish writer, you have to work." He said, "I see now writers coming to me with problems, complaints. I say to them, 'Here I was in a strange country. I made $12 a week when I needed to make $40 and still I wasn't sorry. I did not complain. I did not weep on anybody's shoulder.'"

In my work as a magazine editor, it would have been useful to invite Singer to the office—to serve as a living example for writers who occasionally, or more than occasionally, wept beyond all necessity. As it was, many lessons were drawn from our discussions that I could pass on to all who needed encouragement and advice, which of course turned out to be all my writers, weeping or not.

I told them that Singer, even with his experience and stature, still struggled each day with his work. It was no accident that his stories flowed so naturally and his characters seemed so real. It was the result of planning, changing, and rewriting. I told them the secret of his characters' universal appeal: they must emerge as individuals, not as stereotypes. Just because a man is from Warsaw and has a beard does not mean his name is Goldberg.

I repeated, too, what Singer taught in an occasional writing class at the University of Miami. No two writers are alike, he would say. Nor should they be. There are many kinds of valid writing, many valid ways to compose fiction or nonfiction. "Where is it written that every story must be for a general readership? When Joyce wrote *Finnegans Wake*, he was ready for footnotes. This is a type of writing. Some like it. Some not. There are such writers."

Singer's own writing needs no footnotes, nor could it serve as a proper example of Tom Wolfe's literary manifesto for the modern novel, necessarily rooted in the reporting of man versus his urban environment. It is more gentle—and more savage— than that. Mostly, it is one writer's singular voice. In 1935, when Isaac Bashevis Singer came to America and found work for $12 a week, he could have done better financially by adopting someone else's voice. He chose, under duress, to write his own way. He had no guarantees, only an instinct. No one said to him, "Isaac, you must be singular. You must develop over the next fifty or sixty years a volume of work in which your characters, imperfect in an imperfect world, address their various demons. You must make your stories compelling, human, real, believable; your characters must be the sort that we have met in the street, or in our very houses. You must make us laugh and think and, yes, weep. We must enjoy your stories and also learn from them. This you must do to win a Nobel Prize. This you must do to be a great writer." No, nobody said that. But over time, a great deal of time, and through an undocumentable and enormous effort, and by following the instructions of an inner voice that at times seemed spoken by a demon, Isaac Bashevis Singer took his place among the masters.

It was odd, those days in Miami, going to lunch with a master, walking the streets—even the very street, Ninety-fifth, renamed for him—without a hint of recognition from his fellow residents. To other walkers, Singer, dressed in a sport coat and boater, must have seemed just like any other old man in south Florida. One more Goldberg.

The Nobel Prize had not been the key to great fame. It could not be the payoff. The payoff, Singer would say—and any writer would say—is the delight of writing the words. And then rewriting them and getting them right.

It was easy to discuss with Singer other people's writing. But during our last lunch together before I moved north, we proceeded to the cash register and Singer took his straw hat and put it on his head, and said, "I wanted to talk to you about your writing." I froze. "That piece you wrote last Sunday about your parents," he said. "It was very courageous. Not many writers would have risked such a thing."

Although we corresponded many times, I saw Isaac Bashevis and Alma Singer only once after that. They visited Hartford, where he received an honorary doctorate at the university. It was a rainy day, and Alma was worried that Isaac would catch cold. But he seemed fine, and as he settled down into a couch in the president's living room, I made another pitch for a story. This time, I said, we had no crush of business, plenty of time. He said, "I would be glad to give you a story, my friend." A few weeks later, I received in the mail a lovely piece called "Gifts." It was an appropriate title. Its author had given me many.

ॐ 13 ॐ

Me, Myself, and You

Final Thoughts on Taking Writing Personally

With something less than overwhelming pride, I reprint here the first words I ever wrote for publication. They concerned a zoning dispute between local restaurant owners and mobile food vans. The story in the *Ohio University Post* of September 21, 1961, began:

"There is a reason for the missing sandwich truck on our campus."

Well, now, some mitigation may be offered for what I came to understand was the commitment of a journalistic misdemeanor. I was a freshman in college, my reverence for precise language had not yet developed, and there was no one to advise me in the *Post* offices that the real news would have been that there *wasn't* a reason for the missing sandwich truck on campus. Instead the reaction I received was "Nice story, kid," from an old hand on the staff who may have reached his twentieth birthday.

It took just a few decades for me to understand that the person who issued that charitable observation did not have any honest appraisal of my work on his agenda. His intent was only to encourage me. Even at his age, he knew a universal truth—that writing, no matter how skilled it may eventually become, may never seem good enough. For every positive reaction, there is a negative—or two negatives. Amid such potentially damaging circumstances, the "veteran" was careful to be positive, a not unwelcome attribute in this business.

But then, if colleagues can be unduly encouraging, where do you go for the real truth about your talent? If you have been paying attention to all these chapters, you know the answer already. There is no better critic of your work than the person who wrote it. No one can convince you it is wonderful if you know that your research was weak or your effort at avoiding convention was minimal. In the long run, "Nice work, kid" did not convince me that the way I addressed the sandwich truck issue was the best way to address it. (I should have revealed the reason for the missing truck in the first sentence.) On the other hand, work that you can look back on with genuine satisfaction after a space of time is response enough to the furrowed brows of critics.

As a writer, you must understand that negative reaction should not defeat you, and at the same time you must grow at your craft, which requires paying attention to criticism. If, as I have observed a few times in this document, writing is a spiritual adventure, it demands moving from here to there. That goal in itself can be inspiring and rewarding. Few writers look back on a body of work and think it perfect. In conversations for this book, Jim Ricci commented on his breakthrough Garry Trudeau profile, "I would have written that piece much differently today." Yet such realization didn't diminish the triumph of the moment. The craft of writing is similar to that of painting or composing: there is always something more to say and some better way to say it. There will be those who encourage you and those who will say or write things about your work that will hurt you. You must continue on your journey of words toward that elusive perfect destination, absorbing lessons along the way, unafraid of the critiques, and not too easily satisfied by praise.

This is not to suggest that having an encouraging teacher or editor is not an advantage. When Mr. Edwin Hill announced to my parents that their twelfth grader may not have as black a future in the field of communication as we all might have imagined, my confidence was buoyed—at least long enough to sink into Professor Robert Michael's Freshman English quagmire of required metaphor. "Go, my dear students," he ordered, his right index finger pointed to the ceiling, a smile on his carrot-thin face, "to a local den of iniquity this weekend and return with a metaphor-filled essay that is free—under penalty of failure—of adjective." Mr. Michael decried not only adjectives but *Time* magazine and all slickly packaged words, a campaign that fell on fascinated but confused ears. The professor did not reappear for a second term—the rumor was that students had written home about required attendance in townie bars—but his impressions of language remained. My impressions have included a lifelong search for metaphor devoid of, or minimally encumbered by, adjective, even if the subject is not always inspired by iniquity. Well, "lifelong" overstates the case. The truth is that Ron MacMillan, a more fluent and imaginative writer than I was, had written an inspired English theme for a different professor, a theme that I must have found so perfectly crafted that I borrowed the first paragraph for the final exam. When informed by Mr. Michael that I had failed the test I was surprised. How could he know of my plagiarism? The answer occurred to me only years later. What I wrote, inspired though it might have been, did not reflect my way of thinking or writing. He would have happily awarded a C-plus on the final, a grade to which I aspired, if only I had offered my normally confused syntax, leaving in the margins ample room for the good professor to scribble the inevitable "Awkward."

The final grade in the course was a charitable C-minus, which did not prevent my progression to Freshman Composition and beyond, where I never forgot the lessons of the professor. No matter what I wrote—and no matter how badly—I could at least be assured that no one else would be to blame for it.

ɔɦ ɾʅɔ

Years later, as already described adequately in this book, I became an editor, that scariest of creatures, whose job it is to pass judgment on the work of others. My tendency in this work has been to be a gentle, if demanding, critic. That is, I always try to find something nice to say about pieces I personally reject. This is not hard to do for even the dreariest example. Inevitably there is a spark somewhere, a defensible reason the writer undertook the project. And I know—my own experiences prove it—that writing is a lifetime pursuit, and that any writer, given proper encouragement and honest self-evaluation, cannot help but grow and improve.

I made the decision early in my career that, if my writers had to risk criticism, so would I. My column would appear each week. There were other reasons for this, among them that I wanted the magazine to make a personal connection with readers and I had an undeniable need to become locally famous. And there was also this: my writing was a response to the yearning for personal expression. Although in college I once got a summer job as a tour guide because the proprietor was under the impression that "all Hebrews are good storytellers," I was not a confident speaker; I could not easily express myself in any other way but writing, and that was a chore. Some of my early work was certainly a chore for readers; it was verification of Shakespeare's observation that it was indeed possible to be both brief and tedious.

My earliest columns were written in the fashion of editors' columns. They often told behind-the-scenes tales of how cover stories were reported. But after a few years of this, and when every editor on earth seemed engaged in the same exercise, I asked myself, "As a writer, what do I really have to say?" Oh, a scary thought. It is easier to hide behind the journalistic scenes. But turning thirty helped. And thirty-five. And forty. And forty-five. And, as the years passed, as innocence passed, as more and more of my money went for college tuitions and property taxes and down various rat holes and to lawyers for my own ill-advised performances of everyday life, and as I digested the headlines of the daily newspapers, I began to understand that real life never did get much space in the public print. And as I felt compelled to explore how my own experiences changed my view of the world, I expanded my weekly essay into every area I could think of. Even, eventually, into a very private area. Just a few years ago I described in a metaphorical way (Professor Michael would have approved) a certain examination that every man over the age of forty-five must undergo if he is to maintain some sense of confidence about his health and, particularly, his

colon. Care was taken to describe the procedure delicately, so as
not to offend those who shrink from the very mention of body
parts. From the response I got in the community, it was clear the
readership approved of the column. I had been successful at my
main intent—to encourage men, notoriously private about their
private parts—to make the effort to become medically aware
and to summon the courage to voluntarily undergo uncomfortable or embarrassing procedures that might save their lives.
However, one reader—the man who then happened to be editor, publisher, and chief executive officer of the newspaper—
came to the four o'clock news conference the next day and held
the column aloft by the corner of the page, as if he were finger-
ing a sheet of paper that had been dipped in some vile substance. He exclaimed, "Why do I have to read about Lary
Bloom's asshole?"

The CEO, editor, and publisher had missed the point. I had
taken great care to avoid describing the procedure in an offensive way—metaphor was critical in this effort. I had not
stooped, as he did, to gutter language; nor did I feel as if I had
to defend the piece, or point to his behavior as an example of
how pots refer to kettles. If he missed it, he missed it. The
important point is that I knew what I was trying to say, and I
was satisfied it was said in the best possible manner. This is not
always the case by any means.

An editor who had not written before was about to introduce
a column and asked my advice. I said, "You know, this will
sound funny to you. It seems so obvious. But there is one thing
you must remember in writing. You must have a point, or several points, to make."

You see, I make my living at this—writing and teaching writing—and have done so for a long time, and yet sometimes the
act of writing, or trying to write, sends me into a state of, well,
despair is not too strong a word. "Why, Why?" "What's the
matter?" I want to know. If I have my wits about me that day,
which from the evidence seems doubtful, I can figure out what
is wrong: I have no point. Perhaps I have a funny scene, or a
clever beginning, or some good dialogue. But what am I trying
to say? Aha!

For me, there were two origins for essays that worked. The first was the precise, premeditated point of view. This was the method least often used. That is, I likely would not ask myself, "How do I feel about Ronald Reagan?" and then write a column on my views of the presidency. More often I would draw on a series of events—something that happened that could be described, or some personal circumstance that made an interesting narrative. That is, I always preferred telling a story and then weaving into that story the point, which may seem to have nothing to do with the physical event. If I were writing about a day at a country fair, for example, some comment about Ronald Reagan might slip into it during a description of the pie-eating competition.

Most of my work was in the form of short essays, but that did not mean that they necessarily took a short amount of time to write. Nor was I finished after I had written them. This was useful in teaching other writers.

One fellow who had never written a serious piece for publication dropped off a narrative with these confident words: "It is very good. Everyone I have showed it to says it's perfect. I worked hard on it. Even had to rewrite it once." I said, "You did, eh? One whole time?" (Try as I may I cannot always sidestep sarcasm, especially if it is warranted.) A few days later, when he asked for an assessment of the work, he was taken aback by my view that, although what he had submitted was indeed a good start, it was not necessarily a good finish. I explained that in a narrative more must be offered than a clear, comprehensive detailing of events, that the writer must interpret these events, must offer commentary. The writer must weave description and observation in the same way the great novelists did. He looked at me as if I were saying something revolutionary, as if Mark Twain or Jane Austen or Leo Tolstoy had never existed. I comforted him. And I said that writing is a matter of rewriting, and rewriting. I did not convince him. He left without committing to a second rewrite.

I might have told him—I did not, however—the number of times I rewrote columns, looking for the best possible expression or the right balance. I could have told him how many times

I thought early versions were top-heavy; they offered too much action for the amount of space and thought that went into the conclusion. I could have told him that even when the essays came easily—when they poured out of the word processor as if they were writing themselves—there was the duty even on those glorious days to reexamine the material, to tighten, to polish, to make it more precise.

Those days when the writing came easily were the best days. I felt as if I could write forever, that I would never run out of decently expressed thoughts. Even then I knew I had to go back to the material. And on the next day, too. And on the day after that.

Phyllis Rose says, "The wonder about writing is that it isn't frozen. It can be revised. So be spontaneous. That's important. Get it down. And then don't be afraid to change it. Some people are so surprised they've actually written something good that they think it's sacred."

I know precisely what she means. In my early writing days, whenever a reasonably expressed thought emerged from the typewriter I was impatient to have it published. Eventually it became clear that reasonably expressed was not nearly good enough. The point was driven home simply by time and experience—and once and for all when Stephen Jones wrote the first of many pieces for *Northeast,* an essay about Long Island Sound in the winter. It so happened, as it often occurs in the magazine business, that the printer's deadline proved too imminent for comfort, and I called Steve to check impatiently on progress.

"Oh, the piece is finished," he said in response to my inquiries.

"Good," I said, "put it in the mail."

"I can't."

"Why not?"

"I've got to let it sit on the table awhile to see if it shifts."

"If it what?"

Later, I understood what he meant. A piece never reads the same way the next morning, or the morning after that. Steve always saw things that needed to be changed; words that had been repeated, awkward phrasing, imprecise language, a new metaphor possibility, a different way to make the point. A day or two after the writing, the sense of personal objectivity returns. You read the piece with a fresh, more critical eye.

Shifting, of course, is advised only for a basically sound piece. Something poorly written will sit forever on the dining room table but can never age well; not even an earthquake will help. You should know, if you don't already, that a large percentage of your work, most notably in its early stages, will seem inadequate to you. These are difficult moments. You begin to question your abilities, and whether you have any facility with language. You should know that these feelings are entirely normal. And they can lead to a very common and troublesome state known as writer's block.

I can recall a time very early in my essay days when the work did not come easily. Only a few hours from deadline, I had managed to produce not one reasonable word, only a volume of sweat. I had tried writing about three subjects—but felt empty about them all, as if I had nothing to offer about any one of them that could possibly be of interest.

It was at this vulnerable point that a caring editor stopped by and noted my distress. He did two things. First he put a typesetting code on the word processor. "There," he said. "It always helps to get something on the screen." Then he began talking to me about any subject, anything that would draw a response, an opinion, a glimmer in my eye, until we struck upon something that made me sit up in my chair. That subject was the Anglo's accommodation of the Spanish language, a rich opportunity for any columnist. It was uncharted territory, a place to work out undeveloped feelings about a community around me that did not speak my language.

I was saved. That is, I was able in the next few hours to fill the space acceptably. Years later, when I looked back on that column, it was not with any satisfaction for the writing, which was clumsy—a necessary result of a day of inarticulation and lack of time for rewrite. But I learned that failure on one day to write well is not evidence that the future holds nothing but disaster. You work through it, and you begin to see that some days are better than others. And some days are—I hope Mr. Michael,

wherever he is, will pardon the adjective—wonderful. To succumb to an obvious comparison (and I knew I would succumb
to it somewhere in this book—perhaps you will give me credit
for waiting this long), writing is in this regard not unlike hitting
a baseball. Even the best players hit the ball squarely only a
small percentage of the time. When they do find themselves in
a hot streak, it seems to them as if hitting is easy, that it will
always come easy. But they know better. They know that some
days they will wonder if they will ever again touch first base. In
such cases experience helps. Good baseball players survive the
game because they understand its highs and lows. As a writer
you will play the same game. When you are seasoned, you will
know that no slump, no matter how discouraging or prolonged,
should make you give up. Like a baseball player, you should not
waste time or energy worrying. On bad days, depart for an hour
from the anticipated agenda. Instead of writing the piece, write
a letter to a friend, or a missive of frustration to some business
that caused you grief—something in which the point of view is
obvious. Many times such an exercise will get your writing on
the right track, and you'll turn a bad day into a good one.

When the days are nothing but good, you will very much
enjoy, from a literary point of view, hitting nothing but solid
line drives and home runs. Enjoy them while you can. But never
fear that you'll run out of them. For a time, I hoarded my words.
In the midst of writing an essay, I might say to myself, "Better
slow down—you'll eventually run out of words. Don't use this
anecdote now. You might need it in a couple of years when you
are entirely depleted of thoughts." That's not how to think. The
brain is a remarkable regenerating tool and will continually
produce new thoughts and summon new experiences. Don't be
afraid to spend your currency. Don't be afraid to use your best
stuff.

श्र   ग्ल

It always helps, during times of little production, to remind
yourself what you are doing as a writer: you are looking for
clues, for illuminations, for the surprises of life.

I am always looking for such detail—because in detail I can

find that sense of surprise. The punch line. The illumination of the piece. That "Aha!" factor. It was not always a moment that punched me in the noggin. Yet I came to believe that the combination of positive attitude, attuned eye, and vulnerable heart would yield much greater results than might be imagined.

Not long ago, I wrote a piece for *Northeast* about a young dancer who answered a call for auditions for the road company of the musical *Cats*. I had a strong feeling about how to do the article: I would take the reader through the experience. To make that possible, I would meet the dancer in the days before the audition, learn all I could about her and her hopes, her life, and particulars of her training. My interest in the theater would provide the basis of a perspective, which then could be augmented with research into the realities of this road company. I imagined a compelling narrative with observation about one young woman's attempt to try for the big time. But, as is almost always the case in writing and show biz, plan and actuality parted company.

I found Lisa White to be entirely charming. She had the warm and expressive face of a natural performer and a dancer's grace. She was eloquent both on the subject of dance and on her own expectations. She was certainly a central character who would gain the empathy and support of readers. A dozen years of formal training, the fact that at twenty-seven she probably had only one more chance at a young dancer's game, and that she had never lived up in her own mind to the promise she thought she had were critical points. Readers would root for this professional manicurist to put down her nail polish and apply her greasepaint at last.

A simple narrative seemed to be the answer. Act 1: Meet Lisa. Act 2: The audition and result. Background and perspective could be offered through both acts. No matter what, there would be, as in the theater, a natural climax. Or so I thought.

All went according to plan only until the first lineup of dancers were each asked individually to perform double pirouettes. Although all had danced by this point, it had been only together as a group. That was warm-up. Here was the first part of the real audition. When it came Lisa's turn, she stepped forward with confidence, displayed good posture and stage presence, and twirled into her move. It was perfect, except for the ending; she planted her right leg behind her with less authority than she would have liked. She was asked to try again. Once more, the pirouettes were graceful, until the end. The director, who had not shown great interest in the preceding auditioners, asked Lisa questions, the last of which was "How long have you studied dancing?" She replied, quickly and proudly, "Twelve years."

When after several chorus lines had completed their individual pirouettes, the finalists were selected and asked to stay. My subject, I was surprised and horrified to learn, was not among them. Now my piece had a fatal flaw. The emotional center was Lisa. Already she was gone—packed up and back to her job at the salon. How could I narrate a tale in which the main character was missing from the last half? I knew two things: I had to minimize, without making the piece top-heavy, the physical presence of the final selection process, and I had to figure a way to get Lisa back in the piece.

In the hallway during a break, the casting directors talked of the audition and of auditions past. They spoke of three people they had found this way—real success stories about young performers from the provinces who went on to notable Broadway careers. I filed this information, and knew that I could use it early in the piece as a digression—not as a narrative scene, but simply as information planted early to give readers an indication of what might be possible for the people on stage today. Such an out-of-sequence technique is not cheating. In nonfiction, information may be moved—and often is moved—backward and forward at the convenience of the narrative, as long as it is presented as helpful background and does not mislead, or tell an untruth.

I pressed the director to talk about Lisa. "Why didn't she make it?" The director said that they had been impressed by her. Then they saw her trouble with the double pirouette. This was why they asked how long she had trained. When she said twelve years—as long or longer than any other auditioner—their interest wasn't heightened, as Lisa had anticipated. In fact, they lost

interest. They could work with someone who had limited training and unlimited potential. But Lisa was too far along at the age
of twenty-seven, and too unpolished. There was my narrative's
surprise. There was the "Aha!" factor. In an effort to impress in
the audition, Lisa had been frank about her training. It had,
however, the opposite effect of what she had intended. The
bottom half of my narrative now included Lisa. And it had a
surprise, a kicker to a dance piece—a reward for the reader who
would stick with it.

☙ ❧

In a sense we are all Lisa Whites. Readers of Sunday magazines
who see the possible fulfillment of long-held dreams in her are
not much different from writers who hope that one day they will
be published widely.

The process of writing this book has required devotion and
attention to that universal dream. I have thought a great deal
about writing, and there has been so much I have wanted to say
to you about this rich subject. I wanted you to know, for example, that in the attempt Lisa White made, she found great satisfaction. She grew. She learned. Something was certainly gained.
And in every attempt you make as a writer, you will gain as well.
An advantage you have is that your age is no barrier, unlike that
of a dancer. It becomes, in fact, an advantage as you grow older.

You will find that the act of writing itself is the most rewarding part of a very rewarding field. No doubt seeing your name in
lights—in *Atlantic Monthly* or *The New Yorker* or on the cover of
a book—is a delightful sight, but it is the writing itself that is the
real magic.

I am sometimes asked by various groups what hobbies I
enjoy. And I dutifully list them. I enjoy playing the piano. I play
a less than disastrous round of golf, an activity I have certainly
warmed to. I run. But you have heard enough from, and about,
runners.

These things give me good feelings, but there is nothing that
can match the feeling of writing, and of having written. If there
is one point I can make to you—one that you hold onto long
after you have disregarded my advice about the organization of

a narrative or the particulars of a profile—it is this: write, write, write, and then write some more. There will be bad days. There will be days when you consider yourself a fraud. And there will be days when the magic happens.

ॶ ೧ೕ

Much advice has been given here. Many experts have been cited. And yet the final excerpts here are reserved for a man who wrote but one piece. He is a person I think of when I consider the possibilities, when I think of the natural act that writing is, when I argue that writing is an instinct that should never be denied.

In the fall of 1978, I was invited to lunch to meet Dominic Koo, a municipal court judge in Miami. He was planning a trip to China—his first trip there since leaving to become a law student in Minnesota. Just after Koo departed, in 1949, Mao's troops marched into Shanghai, Koo's hometown, and those who had gone abroad, particularly those who studied capitalist ways, became exiles. So in the effort to educate himself, Dominic Koo had said good-bye to his family, perhaps forever.

I learned, that lunchtime in 1978, that it was not the first time I had heard his name. Just a couple of years earlier, Judge Koo had made news by arresting a fellow grocery shopper who would not heed the store's nonsmoking policy. And years before that, and before appointment to the bench, he had become a national figure of sorts as a contestant on the quiz show "The $64,000 Question." He was one of the most popular guests ever because of his lively personality and the fact that this young man from China was an expert in the category "Americana." He recalled, "The producers actually assigned the subject to me. They thought it would be a good idea to have a man from China answer questions that would stump native-born Americans. So I went to the library, and read and read and read." Dominic Koo memorized thousands of facts, a demonstration of his compulsive nature.

And now he was telling me about his latest compulsion. Or compulsions. Something had come over him, he said. Some notion. Some drive. Some voice in his head told him that now

was the time to act. After thirty years, it was time to go back to
China. It was time to see his mother (his father had died much
earlier). He would do so knowing full well that China's restric-
tive travel terms would not allow him to digress from the official
tour; that the closest the group would come to his mother's
neighborhood would be several miles away; and that any variation by any traveler, particularly if he were native Chinese,
might mean arrest and certainly would mean expulsion from the
tour. The judge was saying, in effect, he was willing to break the
law, even if it was Chinese law, for what he thought would be
the last chance to see his mother, who obviously couldn't even
be informed of his plans, for fear that the authorities would stop
him.

"I have to do it now," he said, "I don't know why. I just
must." And then he said, "I also want to write about it. I have
never written anything, except legal opinions. But I must write
about it."

"Please do," I replied. I told him—as you must suspect by
now—to keep a journal, to simply put down his thoughts as
they occurred to him. And I wished him well.

A couple of weeks later I received a package from Japan, the
first stop on his journey. It contained a long letter from Dominic
Koo in which he brought me up to date on his trip, weaving into
the letter a beautifully detailed account of his Shanghai childhood and the neighborhoods of the cosmopolitan city. This was
described so well I could smell the dishes prepared at his
parents' table, and I could understand the reverence for learning
in his house; I could actually see, in the alley behind the house,
the handwriting on the synagogue walls. In short, I was right
there in the 1940s in China, and I felt the rich promise of return.

Just as it was, I knew this letter would be an ideal beginning
to the piece. "Just keep going, Judge Koo," I prayed. "Just keep
going."

When he returned to the States, he gave me the rest of the
story—a story that needed very little editing. He told of the
journey in straightforward language, in detail. He did not try to
induce sympathy, or to artificially heighten the drama. He
simply told what happened, including his unlawful side trip, for

which he had borrowed a native costume in order to be inconspicuous, and had caught a city bus to the old neighborhood. And then he told about the moment that all readers were waiting for:

> As I climb the stairs, the occupants of the first and second floor come out to peer at me. My first question reveals my identity. "You are Kung's son from America?" A kindly Mrs. Yang, about 50 years old, tells me my mother is not in and that I should come in her apartment for some hot tea. Mrs. Yang explains that my mother usually gets up early for group calisthenics at the Bund Park, takes walks for exercise and enjoys herself at a noodle house for breakfast. I did not know that the kitchen was shared by all the occupants.
>
> Tea is served. While waiting, hot tea is far better than cold drinks. It lasts longer, and relieves my anxiety. Mrs. Yang asks me about the trip, and informs me my mother has recently recovered from a fall and that only one sister of mine (Ching Yah, who was six months old when I left) was staying with her. She says my letters mentioned a trip sometime next year. Mrs. Yang had seen my pictures, and recognized me at first sight. My not-so-eloquent Shanghai accent is getting a workout. But in my heart, I am singing, "Mother, won't you please come home?"
>
> After about 10 minutes, I hear a woman's voice downstairs—weak, flat, indistinct. Within seconds, from the enunciation and tone, I recognize it to be my mother's. First she is incredulous. "Who you say is waiting upstairs? My son from America? No, you mean the mail arrived. This is too early for practical jokes. You say it's for real!" She begins to stutter and her voice becomes shrill.
>
> As she looks up the stairs, she sees the waiting figure, and darting like a young woman, begins to climb. The sight sends a surge of energy through my body. I feel partially paralyzed, my limbs numb and inactive. But I

quickly gather my strength and descend the stairs, telling
her to stand still. My heart is pounding. Those 12 steps
seem like an eternity.

Finally, I stand in front of her. I stretch my arms and
embrace her. Her words are almost inaudible, but
pressed against me, I hear her say, "My son has come
home!" My voice is choking. I try to catch my breath,
which comes in short bursts. Words are unnecessary. I
hold her, pulling her to me, and let out one word between my ragged breaths: "Um-Ma." My Mom!

The effect of the piece was overwhelming. It wasn't only
those who had left relatives behind in China or Cuba or Europe
who responded. It was everyone with a heart, everyone who
understood matters of guilt and of love and of sacrifice and of
forgiveness. Everyone mature enough to sense that life is epic
adventure that necessarily returns us to the values of youth.
Everyone who could feel. It spoke to people who, up until that
day, had retained prejudices for those who were different and
who could now see that foreign cultures were the provinces of
people whose hearts and minds were very much like theirs.

I cannot say that I have a favorite piece after publishing
thousands. But if I had to say so, I would say that this was it—it
spoke to so many, and it was written by a man who had no real
experience as a writer. And there was one other factor that
makes it special and telling—and why it is in the final chapter in
this book.

In the year or so following his story's publication, Judge Koo
and I often met for lunch. I liked him very much, and sought his
opinions on the problems of south Florida. His views were
always keen, and his sense of humor was always at the ready.

Then one lunchtime he was late. This was uncharacteristic of
this punctual man. When he finally arrived, I saw that his face
was pale. "I have been to the doctor," he said. "I have a spot on
my lung." He tried to put it in a good light. He even made a joke
about the irony of a judge who had had a smoker arrested
contracting lung cancer himself. I thought—in the naive way
that we like to think about those with serious disease—that

Judge Koo could beat the rap, that positive spirit would triumph. But cancer is not always impressed by even such extraordinary human characteristics. Six months later, Judge Koo was dead.

At the funeral, the priest remarked about his life and his work. He told the mourners, too, about the judge's trip to China. "Who can forget the remarkable account in *Tropic*?" he asked. "It was as if the trip was preordained. And it was as if we all had taken it with him."

Dominic Koo had listened to the voice in his head. He had listened to it before it was too late.

☽ ☾

During this book's final editing process, Patricia Weiss, a *Northeast* staff writer whose work has been quoted liberally on these pages, urged me to read a piece that had been sent to us reluctantly, a piece that Pat "couldn't put down."

It had been written by a forty-one-year-old woman in the north end of Hartford who, at her husband's urging, had signed up for a few college courses. She had already taken several of them before the school got around to asking for an entrance application, part of which was an essay about aspirations. This woman obviously had chosen to write something different, something risky. It was fiction, but clearly based on the hard realities of life in a city's disadvantaged neighborhoods. What she had written was so moving that her English professor had urged her to submit it to *Northeast*. The student, however, had little confidence in her writing, and feared this would be a fruitless enterprise. It took her two weeks to decide to send the envelope off.

Within a few days of its arrival, several people in the office had read it, and all had praised it. The story featured a woman who took the bus to a posh suburb to clean and maintain the house of a well-to-do family. This character possessed a number of remarkable skills, including a sharp wit and a penchant for making fine baby clothes, and yet she refused to consider herself talented or in any way on the same plane as the rich but shallow family for which she worked.

It was a lovely story—fluent, imaginative, human—and a

metaphor for the aspiring college student, and for all who worry whether they possess redeeming skills.

We called the writer and asked her to come to the office. When she arrived, I asked her if $500 would be acceptable payment for the story. She looked at me as if I were playing a game. "You would pay me?" "Of course," I said. "Around here, we treasure writers. And you are a writer."

Her face was incredulous. "No one ever told me that before," she said, and then she recounted her terror of topic sentences, and of high school teachers, who said she never organized correctly and who evidently convinced her that writing was beyond her reach. *Not so.*

Her husband's encouragement to attend college had helped. Our favorable reaction—and the payment—had certainly helped. But what truly made the difference was within her. The voice. The instinct. The willingness to sit down and put her thoughts on paper.

Perhaps she is still suspicious, still wondering if some fluke allowed her to appear in a magazine. But it is no fluke. It is talent. It is courage.

Her unexpected triumph is a logical end for this book, because it is just the sort of beginning we editors cherish most.